T0102975

English Grammar

Morphology

Dr. Muhammad Ali Alkhuli

Publisher: DAR ALFALAH P. O. Box 818 Swaileh 11910 Jordan Tel & Fax 009626-5411547	الناشر: دار الفلاح للنشر والتوزيع ص. ب 818 صويلح 11910 الأردن هاتف وفاكس 009626-5411547
E-mail: books@daralfalah.com Website: www.daralfalah.com	

بموجب القانون، يُمنع تصوير الكتاب أو أي جزء منه.

English Grammar: Morphology, MA, DA

Copyright: 2010 by the Publisher
All rights are reserved.

No part of this book may be translated, reproduced, stored in a retrieval system or transmitted in any form or by any means, electronic or mechanical, including photocopying and recording, without the prior written permission of the publisher.

2010 Edition

Publisher: DAR ALFALAH **P. O. Box 818** **Swaileh 11910** **Jordan** **Tel & Fax 009626-5411547**	الناشر: دار الفلاح للنشر والتوزيع ص. ب 818 صويلح 11910 الأردن هاتف وفاكس 009626-5411547
E-mail: books@daralfalah.com **Website: www.daralfalah.com**	

رقم الإيداع لدى المكتبة الوطنية
2004/5/1193

425

Alkhuli, Muhammad Ali
    English Grammar: Morphology.
Muhammad Ali Alkhuli. Amman: Dar Alfalah,
2004.
        215 pages
    Deposit No. : 1193/5/2004
    Descriptors: \English Language\
Morphology\\Grammar\

** تم إعداد بيانات الفهرسة والتصنيف الأولية من قبل دائرة المكتبة الوطنية، الأردن.

رقم الإجازة المتسلسل لدى دائرة المطبوعات والنشر 2004/5/1198

ISBN	9 9 5 7 – 4 0 1 – 5 3 – x	(ردمك)

بسم الله الرحمن الرحيم

PREFACE

Most books on grammar emphasize syntax; they either ignore morphology almost completely or give it inadequate attention. Some grammar books, if they deal with morphology, include very few or no morphology exercises. For these reasons, the idea of this book has come into existence and, consequently, this book has become a reality.

The book contains ten chapters. Chapter 1 deals with *word structure*; Chapter 2 deals with *derivation* (prefixes, infixes, suffixes); Chapter 3 discusses *compounding* in detail; Chapter 4 deals with *inflection* in detail; Chapter 5 explains the different means of *word formation*; Chapter 6 deals with *nouns* (forms, types, noun-markers); Chapter 7 focuses on *verbs*; Chapter 8, on *adjectives*; Chapter 9, on *adverbs*; Chapter 10, on *minor word classes*.

In addition to the ten chapters which deal with the internal word structure and word classes, the book contains eight *tables* and thirteen *figures*, most of which summarize the whole chapter which they belong to. Furthermore, the book contains an appendix (Appendix I) for abbreviations used in the book, another appendix (Appendix II) for symbols, and a third appendix (Appendix III) for the symbols of English phonemes.

The book also contains 106 exercises, with 5-17 exercises for every chapter, at the average of one exercise per two pages. The exercises are distributed throughout the sections of the chapter, not at the end of it. There is one exercise at least after each section inside the chapter. Towards the book end, there is a key to the exercises, which can be used by the student to check his answers of each exercise. Finally, the book contains a selected bibliography and a subject index.

It is very important here to remind that this book focuses on morphology, not on syntax, i.e., word structure and the morphological classes of words. Therefore, both the text and exercises focus on words, not on sentences. This book is neither on syntax nor on grammar in general; it is specifically on morphology. Another important point worthy mentioning here is that this book is primarily meant to be a textbook, not an encyclopedia, which includes almost all related units.

Students are advised to do the exercise(s) after each section is dealt with, not after finishing all the entire chapter. Students are also advised not to refer to the "Key to Exercises" except after doing all the exercise; this is essential for making them use the book properly.

I must thank Dr. Jihad Hamdan for his careful reading of the manuscript of this book and for his valuable comments. Finally, I hope that this book will be of use and interest to students of English, to specialists in linguistics and, more specifically, to students of morphology.

Author
Dr. Muhammad Ali Alkhuli

4

CONTENTS

Chapter 3. Compounding 57

Chapter 4. Inflection 71

Contents

List of Tables

List of Figures

CHAPTER 1

WORD STRUCTURE

The smallest meaningless unit in any language is the phoneme. Phonemes string together horizontally or linearly according to certain rules and restrictions and form syllables, which are also meaningless and belong to the phonetic level in language hierarchy. Syllables string together horizontally and make morphemes. **Morphemes** string horizontally to make words, from which we make phrases, clauses, and finally sentences, as shown in Figure 1-1.

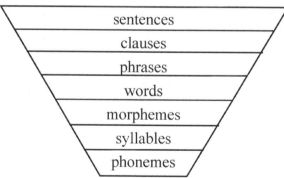

Figure 1-1: Language Hierarchy

Since phonemes and syllables are meaningless, they come under phonetics and thus belong to the phonetic level of language. Since morphemes and words are meaningful, they belong to the **morphological level** of language. Similarly, phrases, clauses, and sentences belong to the syntactic level because they are meaningful and because they require a certain internal order of words.

Therefore, the word comes in between morphemes and phrases: it is higher than the morpheme, but lower than the phrase. The linguistic science which studies the word is called **morphology**, which when combined with syntax makes grammar. Thus, morphology is part of grammar, and so is syntax. Morphology studies the word and its internal structure.

Word Definition

The word (W) is the smallest free meaningful unit in language. Why the smallest? You can find larger units that are free and meaningful, such as the phrase, but the **word** is the smallest unit: you cannot find a unit smaller than the word and free and meaningful at the same time.[1]

The freedom of the word means that the word can stand alone. In slow speech, it may be preceded by silence (or a pause) and followed by **silence**. This silence makes the borders of the word in speech. In writing, a space before and after the word marks its borders and indicates its freedom.

The word has five characteristics. First, it has a meaning. Second, it has a phonemic form, a spoken form, or an audible form, which we can say and hear. Third, it has a written form, spelled form, or visual form, which we use in writing and reading. Fourth, it obeys the phonological rules of the language which it belongs to. Finally, it has grammatical properties and thus belongs to a certain grammatical class, e.g., noun, verb, or article.

Words can be real or potential. **Real words** are actually used and exist in the dictionaries of the language. In contrast, **potential words** obey all the rules of the language although they are not actually used now, nor do they exist in language dictionaries, e.g., *coops, vapy, dasak, citar, molently*. These words look like English words, but none of them is a real word.

In addition, words can be classified into two types. The first type is **underived words** or **simple words**: each word consists of one morpheme only, e.g., *but, and, key, write, go, sit, boy, girl.* The other type is **derived words** or **complex words:** each word has a root plus one affix or more, e.g., *writer, boyish, girlhood, entitles, composition.*

Root and Affixation

A word may be simple or complex. It is **simple** if it consists of one morpheme (M), e.g., *space, mark, in.* It is **complex** if it consists of two morphemes or more. The word *books* has two morphemes: *book+s.* The word *meaningful* has three morphemes: *mean+ing+ful.* The word *meaning-fulness* has four morphemes: *mean+ing+ful+ness.* The word *decentralization* has five morphemes: *de+center+ al+ize+ion.* The word *anti-decentralization* has six morphemes. The maximal number of morphemes in a word can be seven, e.g., *anti-decentralizers: anti+de+center+al+ ize+er+s.*

Each word has a root, e.g., the underlined part in these words: *linguistics, morphology, phonetically, reached, adverb*. Some words have the root only without prefixes or suffixes, e.g., *boy, man, door, chair*.

Thus, the root is essential to the word structure: there is no word without a root. Other morphemes in the word are called **affixes**, which are four kinds:

1. Prefix. It is an affix coming before the root, e.g., *in+clude, con+tain, de+ceive, re+read, dis+trust, im+probable, il+legal*.

2. Suffix. It is an affix coming after the root, whether directly or indirectly, e.g., *come+s, speak+ing, work+er, voice+less, honest+y, home+less, class+ify+ing*.

3. Infix. It is an affix coming inside the root, e.g., *f<u>ee</u>t, t<u>ee</u>th, s<u>a</u>ng, sw<u>a</u>m, sp<u>o</u>ke*.

4. Superfix. It is an affix added on the morpheme. It is usually a primary stress, e.g., *ímport, impórt, éxport, expórt*. Such an affix will not be emphasized in this book since it is not usually considered as a major part of word morphology.

As for the number of morphemes in the word, words are seven types, as shown in Table 1-1:

1.Words with one morpheme, e.g., *table, door, chair, girl, man, can, will*. We may call them **mono-morphemic** words.

2.Words with two morphemes, e.g., *table+s, walk+ed, walk+ing, teach+er, great+er, re+turn*. We may call them **bi-morphemic** words.

3. Words with three morphemes, e.g., *morph+o+logy, lingu+ist+ics, feel+ing+s.* We may call them **tri-morphemic** words.

4. Words with four morphemes, e.g., *pre+pose+ion+s, pur+pose+ful+ness.* We may call them **quadri-morphemic** words.

5. Words with five morphemes, e.g., *pre+mode+ify+ ion+s (=premodifications), post+mode+ify+ion+s (=post-modifications), pro+nomin+al+ize+ion (=pronominal-ization).* We may call them **penta-morphemic** words.

6. Words with six morphemes, e.g., *co+educate+ion+ al+ist+s (=co-educationalists), anti+re+volt+ion+ary+s (=anti-revolutionaries).* We may call them **hexa-morphemic** words.

7. Words with seven morphemes, e.g., *anti+de+ center+al+ize+er+s (=anti-decentralizers).* We may call them **septa-morphemic** words. The maximal word structure is one root plus two prefixes plus four suffixes, as shown in Figure 1-2, which gives the maximal total of seven morphemes in one single word.

Prefix 2	Prefix 1	**ROOT**	Suffix 1	Suffix 2	Suffix 3	Suffix 4

Figure 1-2: Maximal Word Structure

Of course, most words used in language are mono-morphemic, bi-morphemic, or tri-morphemic. The more the number of morphemes in a word is, the less frequent it becomes. Thus, quadri-morphemic words, penta-morphemic words, hexa-morphemic words, and septa-morphemic words are less frequent than words with less morphemes. For a summary of the root and affixes, see Figure 1-2.

Table 1-1: Types of Words

No.	Number of Morphemes (M) in the Word	Word Type
1.	1 M	mono-morphemic
2.	2 M	bi-morphemic
3.	3 M	tri-morphemic
4.	4 M	quadri-morphemic
5.	5 M	penta-morphemic
6.	6 M	hexa-morphemic
7.	7 M	septa-morphemic

Types of Roots

Roots can be classified into two types. The first type is the **changing root**, i.e., a root which shows some change in its pronunciation when an affix is added, e.g., *wide+th→width*, where /ay/ has become /i/. Such changes can be expressed like this:

width   = /wayd/ + /ay→i/ + /θ/
breadth= /browd/ + /ow→e/ + /θ/
length = /lɔŋ/ + /ɔ→e/ + /θ/

More examples are *paths, mouths, baths* (/θ/→/ð/), *children* (/ay/→/i/), *divinity* (/ay/→/i/). These changes are discussed under **morphophonemics**, which studies phonemic changes of morphemes in different environments.

Some grammarians consider these changes as **root allomorphs**. For example, the root *path* has two allomorphs: /pæθ/ for the singular and /pæð/ for the plural followed by /z/.

The second type of roots is the **non-changing root**, e.g., *warm+th→warmth, grow+th→growth.* It is a root whose pronunciation is kept unchanged when affixes are added.

Word and Affixes

As for affixation, words can be of these types:

1. Affixless word. It is a word without affixes; it has the root only, e.g., *can, may, must, to, on.*

2. A word with one prefix or two prefixes, e.g., *re+write, en+rich, be+friend, re+in+force.* It can be called a **prefixed word.**

3. A word with one-to-four suffixes, e.g., *practice+al (=practical), practice+al+ity (=practicality).* It can be called a **suffixed word.**

4. A word with prefixes and suffixes, e.g., *inter+ ject+ion (=interjection), in+differ+ent.* It can be called a prefixed and suffixed word.

5. A word with infixes, e.g., *feet, swam.* It can be called an **infixed word.**

Exercise 1-1

Analyze each word into its morphemes. Example: *underlying = under + lie + ing.*

1. representation   _____   7. communications   _____
2. equality   _____   8. consonants   _____
3. suggested   _____   9. generalization   _____
4. explanatory   _____   10. development   _____
5. speaker   _____   11. Japanese   _____
6. researchers   _____   12. discovery   _____

Exercise 1-2

Analyze each word into prefixes, root, and suffixes; fill in the table as required.

No.	Word	Prefix(es)	Root	Suffix(es)
1.	processed	pro-	cess	-ed
2.	context			
3.	activation			
4.	corresponds			
5.	inflectional			
6.	descending			
7.	syntactic			
8.	interpretation			
9.	position			
10.	unfilled			
11.	information			
12.	dramatically			
13.	specifies			
14.	acceptability			
15.	permissible			

Morpheme and Allomorph

The **morpheme** is the smallest meaningful unit. However, in actual usage, we do not use morphemes; we use morphs. This is similar to the phoneme concept: we do not actually use phonemes; we use phones. The morpheme, like the phoneme, is an abstract concept, which is realized or actualized as a **morph**.

As the phoneme consists of allophones, so does the **morpheme**, which consists of a group of **allomorphs**, which make a family called a morpheme. To illustrate the concept of an allomorph, let us examine the **plurality morpheme** or the plural morpheme, as often called.

Look at these groups of plural nouns:
1. *churches, brushes, judges, buses*
2. *books, bits, jumps*
3. *bags, beds, knobs*

In Group 1, the plurality morpheme is pronounced /ɨz/ because the final sounds of the singular forms are hissing sounds or sibilants, i.e., /s/, /z/, /š/, /ž/, /č/ and /ǰ/. In Group 2, the plurality morpheme is /s/ because the final sound of the singular noun is a voiceless non-sibilant sound like /k, t, p/. In Group 3, the plurality morpheme is /z/ because the final sound of the singular is a voiced non-sibilant sound like /g, d, b/.

Thus, the plurality morpheme has at least three allomorphs phonetically conditioned: /ɨz/, /s/, and /z/. Similarly, the **present morpheme**[2] and the **possessive morpheme** have the same allomorphs. We must notice that not all morphemes have allomorphs, however.

Exercise 1-3

Give the three allomorphs of the possessive morpheme, and show the conditions of their occurrence.

No.	Example	Allomorph	Conditions
1.	George's		
2.	Robert's		
3.	Ali's		

Exercise 1-4

Give the three allomorphs of the present morpheme, and show the conditions of their occurrence.

No.	Example	Allomorph	Conditions
1.	washes		
2.	waits		
3.	swims		

Another example of allomorphs is *the*. Under stress, it is /ðiy/. Before a consonant, it is /ðə/, e.g., *the book*. Before a vowel, it is /ði/, e.g., *the apple*. Thus, *the* has three allomorphs, phonetically conditioned.

There is an important term that goes with allomorphs, i.e., **complementary distribution** (CD). If allomorphs are in complementary distribution, it means that none of them can occur where the others occur. For example, /ɨz/ as a plural allomorph cannot replace /s/ or /z/. Nor can /s/ replace /ɨz/ or /z/. This means that these three allomorphs are in CD.

Another example of allomorphs in CD is the negative morpheme {-in}. This morpheme has several allomorphs phonologically conditioned: / ir /, / il /, / im /, / iŋ /, and / in/. The CD of these allomorphs is this:

1. /ir/ before *r*-initials, e.g., */ir/ + regular*

2. /il/ before *l*-initials, e.g., */il/ + logical*

3. /im/ before bilabials, e.g., */im/ + possible*

4. /iŋ/ before velars, e.g., */iŋ/ + correct (=incorrect)*

5. /in/ elsewhere, e.g., */in/ + direct*

Notice that the above allomorphs are phonologically conditioned and distributed. Such **phonological conditioning** contrasts with **morphological conditioning** or **lexical conditioning** of allomorphs, e.g., *ox+en, child+ren.*

Another related term is **free variation** (FV). If two allomorphs are in FV, it means that either can replace the other. For example, *fish* has two plurals: *fish* and *fishes*. In this case, the Ø allomorph and /ɨz/ are in FV. In addition, words of two pronunciations or more are examples of FV, e.g., *either* pronounced as /ayðər/ or /iyðər/. In brief, the allomorphs of a certain morpheme are either in CD or FV.

Free and Bound Morphemes

If a morpheme can stand alone and can be used alone, it is called a **free morpheme**, e.g., *come, go, sit.* Such a morpheme can function as an independent word. Most roots are free morphemes, but not all of them are so.

Look at these words: *re<u>ceive</u>, de<u>ceive</u>, per<u>ceive</u>, con<u>ceive</u>.* The root in all these words is *ceive,* which is not free: you cannot use it as a free word. Other examples of bound roots and bound morphemes are *sume* in *resume, consume, miss* in *permission, commission, remission,* and *duct* or *duce* in *reduction, conduction, induction, deduction.*

However, all affixes are bound morphemes. They cannot stand alone or be used independently as free words, e.g., *un-, en-, dis-, -ity, -ness, -ment, -ly, -er.*

Exercise 1-5

Is the bold-typed morpheme a root (R) or an affix (A)? Free (F) or bound (B)?

No.	Morpheme	Root or Affix	Free or Bound
1.	norm**ally**		
2.	defini**tion**		
3.	**because**		
4.	ad**ject**ive		
5.	**diffuse**nce		
6.	**semantic**		
7.	**liter**ally		
8.	ac**cord**ance		
9.	choos**ing**		
10.	ar**ound**		

Morpheme and Syllable

Although the morpheme may consist of one syllable only and the syllable may make one morpheme, each of them is different from the other. For example, each of these morphemes consists of one syllable: *make, may, the, see, let, wet, hat, rat.* Each of them is one syllable and one morpheme.

However, some morphemes are made of more than one syllable, e.g., *window, number, simile, stomach.* In fact, a syllable may make one morpheme only, e.g., *hit, cat, go,* or be a part of one morpheme, e.g., *finger, rigid, second.* In some cases, one syllable may make two morphemes, e.g., *books, goes, learned.*

Exercise 1-6

Decide whether each bold-typed syllable makes a single morpheme (SM) or part of a morpheme (PM).

1. nor**mal**	_____	**6.** child**ren**	_____
2. fo**cuses**	_____	**7.** imi**tation**	_____
3. **knowl**edge	_____	**8.** **re**liable	_____
4. adjust**ment**	_____	**9.** whe**ther**	_____
5. ra**ther**	_____	**10.** **error**	_____

A morpheme consists of one syllable or more, but a syllable may make one morpheme or more or be just a part of a morpheme. In some cases, a morpheme may consist of a part of a syllable, e.g., *th* in *warmth*.

Morpheme and Word

A morpheme may make one word, e.g., *door, wall, house, car, tree, fruit*. This is the case if the morpheme is a free one.

However, if the morpheme is not free, it cannot make a word, e.g., *ex-, un-, in-, dis-, mis-, -ness*. These are morphemes, but none of them can make a word. On the other hand, the word must consist of one morpheme at least, and in many cases of more than one morpheme.

There are at least three differences between a morpheme and word:

1. The word can sometimes be divided into smaller meaningful units, e.g., *misuse* (=*mis+use*), and cannot sometimes be divided, e.g., *chair*. In contrast, the morpheme, being the smallest unit, is always indivisible into smaller meaningful units.

2. Not every morpheme makes a word, e.g., *-ity, -er, -ous*. In contrast, every word includes one morpheme or more, e.g., *late, lateness.*

3. The morpheme may be free or bound, e.g., *book, en-*, whereas the word, by definition, is always free.

Exercise 1-7

Analyze each word into its morphemes, and determine how many morphemes (M) it has.

No.	Word	Morphemes	Number of Morphemes
1.	prefixes	pre+fix+es	
2.	expressions		
3.	envious		
4.	conversational		
5.	dependence		
6.	interpersonal		
7.	emphatic		
8.	restrictive		
9.	shorten		
10.	undrinkable		

Root and Stem

Each word has a root. Often, a number of words may have the same root, e.g., *phone, phoneme, phonetic, phonetics, allophone, phonemics, phonology*. All these words have *phone* as a common root. The rule here may look like this:

WORD minus AFFIXES = ROOT

However, the root is something different from the **stem** or **base**. The stem is the word to which we add an affix. For example, the stem of *realize* is *real*, but the stem of *realization* is *realize*. The rule here may look like this:

WORD minus the LAST AFFIX =BASE (or stem)

Exercise 1-8

Identify the root and the stem or base of each word.

No.	Word	Root	Stem (Base)
1.	carelessness		
2.	psychological		
3.	derivational		
4.	inflection		
5.	larger		
6.	subjectivity		
7.	denotation		
8.	actualized		
9.	actualize		
10.	actual		

Notice that if the word has one affix, its root and stem will be identical, e.g., *export, largeness*. If the word has more than one affix, the root will be different from the stem. For example, the root of *modernization* is *modern*, but the stem is *modernize*.

Types of Morphemes

Morphemes are of several types. As for freedom, they are two types: **free** and **bound**. Most roots are free, but some are bound, e.g., *ceive* in *receive*. All affixes, on the other hand, are bound. As for word structure, morphemes are two types as well: **roots** and **affixes**.

As for function and meaning, morphemes are three types. The first type is the **semantic morpheme**. It is that morpheme which has a clear meaning. In fact, most morphemes belong to this type. However, a few phonemes belong to the other two types.

The second type is the **grammatical morpheme**, e.g., the infinitive marker, namely, *to*. The morpheme *to* in *He wanted to go* has no meaning, but it has a grammatical function, hence called a grammatical morpheme. Another example is the conjunction *that* in *He said that he would come*. Another example of the grammatical morpheme is the third person singular present morpheme in words like *goes, does, comes*. Such a morpheme has a grammatical function only.

The third type of morphemes is the **stem-formative morpheme,** which also has no meaning, e.g., *speed+o+ meter, therm+o+meter*. The morpheme *o* has prepared the stem to receive the other component. Such a morpheme is also called an **empty morpheme** or an **empty formative**, e.g., *sensual, factual*.

Notice that some words have a **zero morpheme** or **unmarked morpheme**, e.g., the singularity morpheme in *boy, chair, car*. Another example is the masculine morpheme versus the feminine morpheme, e.g., *lion/lioness, actor/actress, host/hostess*.

Compounds

In most cases, a word is made of a root only or a root and one affix or more. However, some words are made of two words, e.g., *blackboard, football, tablecloth*. Such words are called **compounds** or **compound words**. Thus, a word is of three types: it is **simple** if it consists of the root only, e.g., *street*. Secondly, it is **complex** if it consists of the root plus one affix or more, e.g., *ability*. Thirdly, it is a compound word if it consists of more than one word, usually two, e.g., *classroom*.

Exercise 1-9

What is the type of each word: simple (S), complex (CX), or compound (CD)? Show the morphemic components of the word whether it is complex or compound.

No.	Word	Word Type	Components
1.	grammatical	CX	grammar + ical
2.	call		
3.	outdoor		
4.	pronounced		
5.	permit		
6.	submit		
7.	volley ball		
8.	kind-hearted		
9.	broad-minded		
10.	icy cold		

Homophones and Homographs

Some words are identical in pronunciation, but different in meaning, spelling, or both. They are called **homophones** or **homonyms**, e.g., *I/eye, see/sea, buy/by, ate/eight, some/sum, hour/our, sun/son*.

On the other hand, some words are identical in spelling, but different in pronunciation, spelling, or both. They are called **homographs**, e.g., *use* (V)/ *use* (N), *lead* (V)/ *lead* (N), *read* (present)/ *read* (past), *he'd* (*he had*)/ *he'd* (*he would*), *he's* (*he is*)/*he's* (*he has*), *mine* (*pronoun*)/ *mine* (N). Notice that some of these homographs are homophones as well.

Footnotes

1. The only exception is the case when a word consists of one morpheme. Here both of the two terms overlap and become equally free and minimal.

2. The full term of "the present morpheme" is "the third person singular present morpheme". In this book, the author often uses the short term for the sake of brevity.

CHAPTER 2

AFFIXATION

The most important process in word formation is **affixation** or **derivation**, where one affix or more are added to the root to make new words. The added affix may be a prefix, infix, or suffix, e.g., *enlarge, teeth, widen,* respectively. Let us see how this process may go.

Affixes are two types: neutral and non-neutral. **Neutral affixes** do not have a phonological effect on the base, e.g., *-less* and *-ness* in words like *hármless, pówerless, páperless, sériousness, alértness, ábstractness,* where the base has remained as it is with no change at all.

On the other hand, **non-neutral** affixes cause some change in the consonants, vowels, or stress location in the base. Look at these examples: *translation, erosion, natural, divinity, grammárian,* and *medical,* which are derived from *translate, erode, nature, divine, grámmar,* and *medicine,* respectively.

Prefixes

Here is a list of the most frequent prefixes in English. The prefix, being a morpheme, has its own meaning, which appears in the list. Every prefix is added before a certain root, not any root. Some prefixes are added to nouns, e.g., *bi+cycle,* some to verbs, e.g., *pre+define,* and some to

29

adjectives, e.g., *in+relevant (=irrelevant)*. However, many prefixes can be added to different word classes. For example, *super-* may be added to verbs, adjectives, and nouns, e.g., *superimpose, supernatural, superintendent,* respectively.

Every prefix has a derivational rule, which shows the class to which the prefix may be added and the class of the output. For example, *deci-* is added to a noun to make another noun: *deci*+N→N, e.g., *decimeter*.

In most cases, the prefix does not change the class of the stem; the noun remains a noun, and so does the verb or the adjective, e.g., *re+production, over+eat, il+legal*. In contrast, in some cases, the prefix causes a change in the base class, e.g., *en+rich,* where the adjective has become a verb.

Let us see the most common prefixes in English, their meanings, the derivational rule of each, and some examples in Table 2-1 .

Table 2-1: English Prefixes

No	Prefix	Meaning(s)	Derivational Rule(s)	Example(s)
1.	*ante-*	before	*ante* + V → V *ante* + N → N *ante* + Adj → Adj	*antedate* *anteroom* *antenatal*
2.	*anti-*	against	*anti* + N → N *anti* + Adj → Adj	*anti-Semite* *anti-Semitic*
3.	*arch-*	first, main	*arch* + N → N	*archbishop*

Table 2-1: Continued

No	Prefix	Meaning(s)	Derivational Rule(s)	Example(s)
4.	*be-*	make, treat like	be + Adj → V be + N → V	*becalm* *befriend*
5.	*bi-*	two, coming twice	bi + Adj → Adj bi + N → N	*bilingual* *biplane, bicycle*
6.	*co-*	together	co + N → N co + V → V	*co-author* *co-operate*
7.	*de-*	decrease, take away	de + V → V de + N→V	*de-emphasize* *dethrone*
8.	*deci-*	one tenth	deci + N → N	*decigram, decimeter*
9.	*demi-*	half	demi + Adj → Adj demi + N → N	*demi-official* *demigod*
10.	*dis-*	not	dis + N → V dis + Adj → Adj dis + V → V	*discourage* *dishonest* *disapprove*
11.	*ex-*	former, out	ex + N → N ex + V → V	*ex-wife* *export*
12.	*fore-*	ahead, front	fore + N → N fore + V → V	*forehead* *forecast*
13.	*hect-*	one hundred	hect + N → N	*hectometer, hectoliter*
14.	*hydro-*	liquid, water	hydro + N → N hydro + Adj → Adj hydro + V → V	*hydrophobia* *hydrostatic* *hydroanalyze*
15.	*in-*	not	in + N → N in + Adj → Adj	*inability* *inaccurate*
16.	*kilo-*	one thousand	kilo + N → N	*kilogram, kiloton*

Table 2-1: Continued

No	Prefix	Meaning(s)	Derivational Rule(s)	Example(s)
17.	*mal-*	bad, badly	$mal + N \rightarrow N$ $mal + Adj \rightarrow Adj$	*maladjustment* *maladjusted*
18.	*micro-*	very small, one millionth, local	$micro + N \rightarrow N$ $micro + Adj \rightarrow Adj$	*microscope* *microscopic*
19.	*milli-*	one thousandth	$milli + N \rightarrow N$	*millimeter*
20.	*mis-*	badly, wrongly	$mis + V \rightarrow V$ $mis + N \rightarrow N$ $mis + Adj \rightarrow Adj$	*misunderstand* *miscalculation* *misused*
21.	*multi-*	many	$multi + N \rightarrow N$ $multi + Adj \rightarrow Adj$	*multimillionaire* *multicultural*
22.	*non-*	not	$non + N \rightarrow N$ $non + Adj \rightarrow Adj$	*nonintervention* *nonrigid*
23.	*pan-*	of all	$pan + N \rightarrow N$ $pan + Adj \rightarrow Adj$	*Panhellenism* *pan-Islamic*
24.	*poly-*	many	$poly + N \rightarrow N$ $poly + Adj \rightarrow Adj$	*polygamy* *polygamous*
25.	*post-*	after, behind	$post + N \rightarrow N$ $post + V \rightarrow V$ $post + Adj \rightarrow Adj$	*pos-graduate* *post-test* *post-secondary*
26.	*pre-*	before	$pre + N \rightarrow N$ $pre + V \rightarrow V$ $pre + Adj \rightarrow Adj$	*pre-school* *pre-test* *pre-secondary*
27.	*pro-*	front, siding with	$pro + N \rightarrow N$ $pro + Adj \rightarrow Adj$	*pro-leg* *pro-American*
28.	*pseudo-*	false, falsely	$pseudo + N \rightarrow N$ $pseudo + Adj \rightarrow Adj$	*pseudofoot* *pseudo-classic*

The previous table (Table 2-1) shows only twenty-eight prefixes to the exclusion of many others such as *re-*, *radio-*, *semi-*, *sub-*, *super-*, *tele-*, *trans-*, *tri-*, *mono-*, *ultra-*, *un-*, *vice-*, *con-*, and *en-*.

Exercise 2-1

Analyze these words, showing the prefix, the root, and the meaning of the prefix as well.

No.	Word	Prefix	Root	Prefix Meaning
1.	archangel			
2.	belittle			
3.	bilateral			
4.	co-pilot			
5.	de-value			
6.	disadvantage			
7.	ex-ruler			
8.	forefoot			
9.	hydroscope			
10.	unacceptable			

Exercise 2-2

Analyze these words, showing the prefix, its meaning, root, and the derivational rule. You may refer to the dictionary to check the prefix meaning.

No.	Word	Prefix	Prefix Meaning	Root	Derivational Rule
1.	re-write	re-	again	write	$re + V \rightarrow V$
2.	radio-active				
3.	semi-circle				
4.	hemisphere				
5.	subnormal				

No.	Word	Prefix	Prefix Meaning	Root	Derivational Rule
6.	supernatural				
7.	telescope				
8.	transform				
9.	triangle				
10.	ultraviolet				
11.	unjust				
12.	vice-manager				
13.	endanger				
14.	encircle				
15.	inadequate				
16.	aboard				
17.	ablaze				
18.	anormal				

Exercise 2-3

Analyze these words, showing the prefix and the root, and give the derivational rule of each. Example: *re- write = re + V→V*

No	Word	Prefix	Root	Derivational Rule
1.	immovable			
2.	irregular			
3.	malnutrition			
4.	microfilm			
5.	milliliter			
6.	misbehave			
7.	multinational			
8.	non-human			
9.	polyglot			
10.	post-reading			

There is a difference between a prefix in a complex word and a word in a compound word. For example, *grand* in *grandson* is not a prefix; it is a word in a compound. So is *in* in *inbreeding*. The test of this difference is this: If the unit under test can be free, it is a word, not a prefix. If the unit cannot be free, it is a prefix.

A unit may sometimes be a prefix with a certain meaning, but a word, i.e., not a prefix, with another meaning. For example, *in-* is a prefix in *inability* because it means "not", whereas *in* is a word in *inborn* because it means "in".

Exercise 2-4

Identify the root, and decide if the pre-unit, i.e., the unit before the root, is a prefix (P) or a word (W). What is the type of the whole word: a compound word (CD) or complex word (CX)?

No.	Word	Root	Pre-unit Type: Prefix or Word	Word Type: Compound or Complex
1.	by-root			
2.	company			
3.	over-anxiety			
4.	telegraph			
5.	inbleeding			
6.	inefficient			
7.	self-learning			
8.	under-developed			
9.	grandfather			
10.	antimagnetic			

Types of Prefixes

Prefixes may be classified according to their meaning or function into these types:

1. Negative prefixes like *un-, non-, in-, dis-, a-*, e.g., *unfair, non-smoker, incorrect, dishonest, anormal.*

2. Reversative prefixes like *un-, de-, dis-*, e.g., *untie, defrost, disconnect.*

3. Pejorative prefixes like *mis-, mal-, pseudo-*, e.g., *mishear, malformed, pseudo-intellectual.*

4. Prefixes of degree or size like *arch-, out-, super-, sub-, over-, under-, hyper-, ultra-, mini-*, e.g., *archbishop, outlive, supernatural, subnormal, oversleep, underachievement, hypersensitive, ultra-modern, mini-bus.*

5. Prefixes of attitude like *co-, counter-, anti-, pro-*, e.g., *co-pilot, counteract, anti-social, pro-European.*

6. Locative prefixes like *super-, sub-, inter-, intra-, trans-*, e.g., *superstructure, submarine, international, intranational, transplant.*

7. Prefixes of time and order like *fore-, post-, ex-, re-*, e.g., *foretell, preface, post-secondary, ex-husband, reread.*

8. Number prefixes like *uni-, mono-, bi-, di-, tri-, multi-, poly-*, e.g., *unilateral, monolingual, bilingual, ditransitive, trisyllabic, multisyllabic, polygamy.*

9. Conversion prefixes like *be-, en-, a-*, which change the word class, e.g., *befriend, belittle, bewitch, enrich, enslave, afloat.*

Exercise 2-5

Underline the prefix in each word, and show its meaning and type. The type of the prefix should be one of the nine mentioned in the previous section.

No.	Word	Prefix Meaning	Prefix Type
1.	unexpected		
2.	anti-missile		
3.	pro-religious		
4.	overconfident		
5.	disallow		
6.	mislead		
7.	supermarket		
8.	infrastructure		
9.	dislike		
10.	misinform		

Exercise 2-6

Underline the prefix in each word, and show its meaning and type. The type of the prefix should be one of the nine mentioned in the previous section.[1]

No.	Word	Prefix Meaning	Prefix Type
1.	semi-circle		
2.	review		
3.	undercook		
4.	mini-market		
5.	bilateral		
6.	enlarge		
7.	pre-war		
8.	triangle		
9.	becalm		
10.	interaction		

Suffixes

A suffix, as mentioned earlier, is an affix added after the root. The maximum number of suffixes allowed in one word in English is four. A suffix is added to the root according to certain restrictions. Some suffixes are added to nouns only, to verbs only, to adjectives only, or to more than one class. Remember that every suffix has a meaning and a derivational rule.

Table 2-2 shows a group of English suffixes, their meanings, their derivational rules, functions, and examples.

Table 2-2: English Suffixes

No	Suffix	Meaning	Derivational Rule	Function	Example
1.	*-able* *-ible*	*can be, having*	V + *able* → Adj N + *able* → Adj	Adj-forming	*drinkable* *terrible*
2.	*-al*	*related to*	N + *al* → Adj	Adj-forming	*national*
3.	*-an*	*related to*	N + *an* → $\left\{\begin{array}{l} N \\ Adj \end{array}\right\}$	N-forming Adj-forming	*historian* *African*
4.	*-ence* *-ance*	*act of*	V + *ence* → N	N-forming	*dependence* *disturbance*
5.	*-ent*	*doer*	V + *ent* → $\left\{\begin{array}{l} N \\ Adj \end{array}\right\}$	N-forming Adj-forming	*president* *dependent*
6.	*-dom*	*state of, land of*	$\left\{\begin{array}{l} Adj \\ N \end{array}\right\}$ + *dom* → N	N-forming	*freedom* *kingdom*
7.	*-en*	*give, make*	$\left\{\begin{array}{l} Adj \\ N \end{array}\right\}$ + *en* → V	V-forming	*widen* *strengthen*
8.	*-en*	*made of*	N + *en* → Adj	Adj-forming	*wooden, golden*

Table 2-2: Continued

No	Suffix	Meaning	Derivational Rule	Function	Example
9.	-er	*more* *doer* *citizen in*	Adj + er → Adj V + er → N N + er → N	Adj-forming N-forming N-forming	*larger* *worker* *Londoner*
10.	-ery	*place of, state of*	N + ery → N	N-forming	*bakery, slavery*
11.	-ese	*language of, citizen of, related to*	N + ese → $\left\{\begin{array}{l} N \\ Adj \end{array}\right\}$	N-forming Adj-forming	*Japanese Chinese*
12.	-ess	*female of*	N + ess → N	N-forming	*lioness, tigress*
13.	-ful	*having, quantity that fills*	N + ful → $\left\{\begin{array}{l} Adj \\ N \end{array}\right\}$	Adj-forming N-forming	*careful* *handful*
14.	-hood	*stage, group of*	N + hood → N	N-forming	*manhood, neighborhood*
15.	-ic -ical	*related to*	N + ic(al) → Adj	Adj-forming	*economic political*
16.	-ify	*make*	$\left\{\begin{array}{l} N \\ Adj \end{array}\right\}$ + ify → V	V-forming	*solidify simplify*

The previous table (Table 2-2) shows only sixteen suffixes, but there are many others such as *-ing, -ish, -ist, -itis, -ize, -less, -ly, -ment, -most, -ness, -ous, -ship, -ion, -y, -wise, -ity,* and *-tude.*

Exercise 2-7

Analyze these words, showing the final suffix, its meaning, its derivational rule, and its function.

No.	Word	Final Suffix	Suffix Meaning	Derivational Rule	Function
1.	swimming	-ing	action	V + ing → N	N-forming

No.	Word	Final Suffix	Suffix Meaning	Derivational Rule	Function
2.	childish				
3.	modernism				
4.	linguist				
5.	greenish				
6.	pianist				
7.	appendicitis				
8.	realize				
9.	waterless				
10.	weekly				
11.	quickly				
12.	movement				
13.	whiteness				
14.	dangerous				
15.	friendship				
16.	dictation				
17.	windy				
18	clockwise				
19.	modernity				
20.	purify				

Notice that suffixes do not always change the class of the stem. The suffix *-ous*, for example, changes *danger*, which is a noun, into *dangerous*, which is an adjective. In contrast, *-ish* does not change the class of *green* when it becomes *greenish* since both are adjectives.[2] However, most suffixes change the class of the stem, and very few of them do not cause a change in the class.[3] Thus, suffixes contrast with prefixes in this respect, most of which cause no change in the class.

Exercise 2-8

Analyze these words showing the stem, the last suffix, class of the stem (N, V, Adj, Adv), and class of the whole word (N, V, Adj, Adv).

No	Word	Stem (= Base)	Last Suffix	Stem Class	Word Class
1.	Chinese	China	-ese	N	N
2.	artistic				
3.	glorify				
4.	boyish				
5.	idealism				
6.	tonsillitis				
7.	harmless				
8.	monthly				
9.	psychologist				
10.	smallness				
11.	muddy				
12.	admission				

Types of Suffixes

Suffixes can be classified in several ways. First, one way to classify suffixes is to consider the effect of the suffix on the stem class: Does it change the class of the stem or not? Some suffixes change the class, e.g., *widen* (Adj→V), *simplicity* (Adj→N), *boyish* (N→Adj), whereas some suffixes do not cause a change in the class, e.g., *kingship* (N→N), *botanist* (N→N). Thus, we can classify suffixes into two types here: suffixes causing a **class change** and suffixes causing no class change.

Second, one may classify suffixes in another way. Some suffixes close the word and do not allow other suffixes to come after them, e.g., *larger, largest, books,*

Ali's, speaking, and *learned.* Such suffixes are called **inflectional suffixes**, which are only eight in number. On the other hand, some suffixes do not close the word and allow other suffixes to follow them, e.g., *-less* in *harmlessness, -ize* in *actualization, -ment* in *movements.* Suffixes that are not inflectional are called **derivational suffixes**. For more details on the differences between inflectional and derivational suffixes, see Chapter 4. The difference mentioned here is not a distinctive one; it is just one of many other differences.

Third, suffixes can be classified with regard to their effect on pronunciation. Does the suffix affect the pronunciation of the stem or not? Some suffixes have such an effect, and some do not. Look at these examples in Table 2-3.

Table 2-3: Affixes and Pronunciation

No.	Suffix	Example	Change
1.	*-ity*	sane + ity → sanity	/ey/ → /æ/
		público + ity → publícity	• /k/ → /s/ • stress shift
2.	*-y*	démocrat + y → demócracy	• /t/ → /s/ • stress shift
3.	*-ial*	part + ial → partial	/t / → /š/
4.	*-ize*	public + ize → publicize	/k/ → /s/
5.	*-ion*	dictate + ion → dictation	/t/ → /š/
6.	*-ness*	large + ness → largeness	no change
7.	*-less*	hair + less → hairless	no change
8.	*-ful*	care + ful → careful	no change
9.	*-ly*	quick + ly → quickly	no change
10.	*-er*	teach + er → teacher	no change

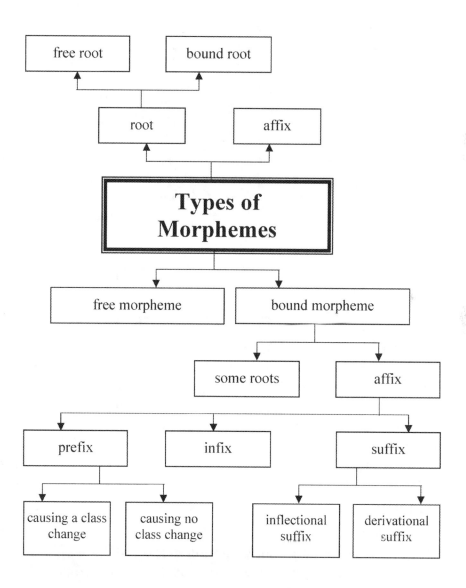

Figure 2-1: Types of Morphemes

Exercise 2-9

Identify the last suffix, then decide whether it changes the stem class or not (Yes, No), whether it is inflectional (I) or derivational (D), and whether it affects the pronunciation of the stem or not (Yes, No).

No	Word	Last Suffix	Class Change	Inflectional or Derivational	Pronunciation Effect
1.	writes				
2.	geographical				
3.	assignment				
4.	syllables				
5.	thinker				
6.	whiten				
7.	greatness				
8.	comprehensible				
9.	rightist				
10	hotter				

Concerning stress, suffixes are of three types. First, some suffixes have no effect on the stress position in the base or stem, e.g., *-ism, -less, -ness*, in *módernism, wáterless, ábstractness*. Second, some suffixes shift the stress to the syllable before them, and they are called **pre-accenting suffixes,** e.g., *history→histáric, Méndel→Mendélian, grammar→grammárian*. Third, some suffixes shift the base stress to themselves, and they are called **auto-stressed suffixes**, e.g., *payeé, examineé, employeé, traineé*. For a summary of the types of morphemes and suffixes, see Figure 2-1 and Figure 2-2.

There is, in addition, a phonological rule that explains some vowel changes in the base. This rule is called the **trisyllabic laxing rule**: If a suffix is added to a word and thus makes it a word of three syllables or more, the tense vowel (a long vowel or a diphthong) becomes a lax (short) vowel. Examples are:

> *div**i**ne* + *ity* → *div**i**nity*   : /ay→i/
> *n**a**ture* + *al* → *n**a**tural*   : /ey→æ/
> *v**ai**n* + *ity* → *v**a**nity*   : /ey→æ/

There is another phonological rule that explains some consonantal changes in the base. This rule is called the **rule of velar softening**. According to this rule, /g/ becomes /ĵ/ before a front vowel, e.g., *analogue→analogy, rigour →rigid*. In addition, /k/ becomes /s/ before a front vowel, e.g., *critic→criticism, medical→medicine, electrical→ electricity*.

Functions of Suffixes

Suffixes can perform a variety of functions:

1. Each suffix surely adds to or changes the meaning of the stem. No stem remains with the same meaning after a suffix is added to it, in almost all cases. The only exception is the grammatical suffix, of course, e.g., the present morpheme in *learn+s*.

2. Some suffixes, i.e., the inflectional ones, close the word and allow no more suffixes to follow, e.g., *walked, walks, walking, larger, largest, books.*

3. Some suffixes form new classes, e.g., a class different from that of the stem. Each suffix marks a certain class. We can call such a suffix a **class-marker** or a **class-formative**. In this regard, suffixes may be as such:

  a. Noun-markers, e.g., *driv**er**, red**ness**, child**hood***

  b. Adjective-markers, e.g., *cloud**y**, advantag**eous**, honor**able**, plant**less***

c. **Verb-markers**, e.g., *black<u>en</u>, ideal<u>ize</u>*

d. **Adverb-markers**, e.g., *clock<u>wise</u>, back<u>ward</u>, active<u>ly</u>*

Exercise 2-10

What kind of marker is each underlined suffix: N-marker, Adj-marker, V-marker, or Adv-marker?

1. relation<u>ship</u>   _____ 9. poet<u>ess</u>   _____

2. politic<u>al</u>   _____ 10. magnet<u>ize</u>   _____

3. teach<u>able</u>   _____ 11. natural<u>ism</u>   _____

4. great<u>ness</u>   _____ 12. hesitat<u>ion</u>   _____

5. applic<u>ant</u>   _____ 13. coast<u>wise</u>   _____

6. prince<u>dom</u>   _____ 14. nation<u>wide</u>   _____

7. kindheart<u>ed</u>   _____ 15. east<u>ward</u>   _____

8. tight<u>en</u>   _____ 16. regular<u>ity</u>   _____

Intra-word Order

As words take a certain order inside the sentence, so do the root and affixes inside the word. Of course, prefixes come first, followed by the root, which is followed by suffixes. However, if two prefixes come before a certain root, they show a certain order of occurrence, e.g., *re-combine*, not **com-rebine*.

Similarly, if two, three, or four suffixes come after the root, they show a certain order as well, e.g., *center+al+ize+ion (=centralization)*, not in any other order, e.g., **center+ize+al+ion,* or **center+ion+al+ize.*

Thus, the order of morphemes inside the word is obviously rigid, without any flexibility. This rigidity clearly contrasts with a certain degree of flexibility shown by words inside a sentence.

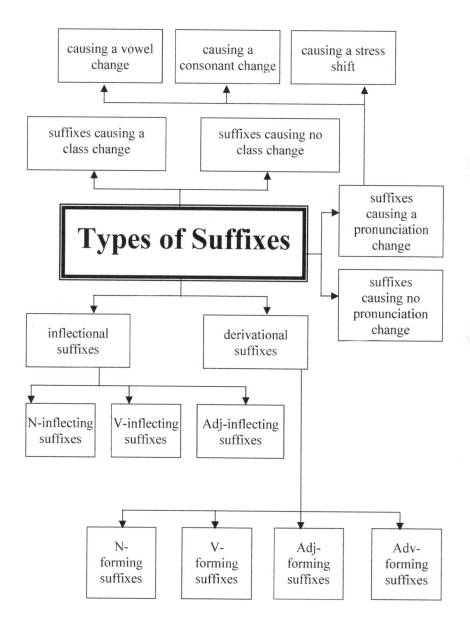

Figure 2-2: Types of Suffixes

Exercise 2-11

Re-arrange these morphemes, e.g., roots and affixes, to make real words, making any necessary changes in spelling.

1. ical + paradox + ly   _____
2. ize + segment + al   _____
3. ed+ broad + mind   _____
4. cook + over + ed   _____
5. ply + im + ion   _____
6. cede + pre + ing   _____
7. s + fere + in + ence   _____
8. ion + clude + in   _____
9. ion + clude + ex   _____
10. fabricate + pre + ion   _____
11. t + strain + con + s   _____
12. ion + al + con + verse _____
13. al + text + con   _____
14. lingu + ics + ist + para _____
15. struct + con + re + ion _____
16. al + ion + anti + ize + globe _____
17. nounce + pro + ion + mis _____
18. municate + mis + ion + con _____
19. ity + non + grammar + ical _____
20. ion + inter + al + nation + ize _____

Infixes

Infixes differ from prefixes and suffixes in that for infixing we do not add an affix, but it is rather a process of **replacement**, whereas for prefixing and suffixing we actually add an affix. For example, in *begin→began*, /æ/ replaces /i/, and no affix is added. We may say that /i→æ / is another allomorph of the past morpheme.

In fact, most irregular verbs require infixes or **replacives** to change the present form to the past form.

Examples are *ride→rode, write→wrote, sing→sang, grow →grew, grind→ground, give→gave, see→saw, speak →spoke.*

The same thing is true about irregular plurals, e.g., *tooth→teeth, foot→feet, louse→lice, mouse→mice, goose →geese.* It is a matter of replacement, not addition.

Exercise 2-12

Show the infix, i.e., the replacive allomorph, in each following case. Example: *foot, feet, /u → iy/.*

1. mouse, mice	_____	**7.** come, came	_____
2. arise, arose	_____	**8.** dig, dug	_____
3. become, became	_____	**9.** draw, drew	_____
4. behold, beheld	_____	**10.** drink, drank	_____
5. bleed, bled	_____	**11.** bind, bound	_____
6. choose, chose	_____	**12.** hide, hid	_____

Complex Derivation

Derivation in word build-up is not always a single process within each word. It may be a repeated process with a multi-layer outcome. For example, let us examine the word *re-activation*. To begin with, the root is *act*. Add *-ive* to get *active*. Then add *-ate* to get *activate*. Then add *-ion* to get *activation*. Then add *re-* to get *reactivation*.

The term **complex derivation** applies to words including two affixes or more. Thus, it is sometimes called **multiple affixation**, e.g., *contradictoriness* (*contra+dict+ory+ness*).

We can express this process in brackets like this, using the **bracketed diagram**:

$$\left(\left[re \right] + \left[\left[\left[\left[act \right] + \left[ive \right] \right] + \left[ate \right] \right] + \left[ion \right] \right] \right)$$

We may use **labeled brackets** to show the levels of derivation and the class of each base in a clear way instead of unlabelled brackets.

$$\left(\left[re + \left[\left[\left[act \right]_V + ive \right]_{Adj} + ate \right]_V \right]_V + ion \right]_N$$

The process can also be represented by labeling without bracketing or with minimal bracketing to accommodate prefixes, e.g.,

$$\left(re + \left[act_V + ive_{Adj} + ate_V \right] + ion_N \right)_V$$

OR

$$\left(re + \left[act_V + ive_{Adj} + ate_V + ion_N \right] \right)_N$$

We may also express the process this way, using the **box diagram**:

re	act	ive	ate	ion	N
	act	ive	ate	ion	N
	act	ive	ate	V	
	act	ive	Adj		
	act	V			

We may express it in another way, using the **tree diagram**:

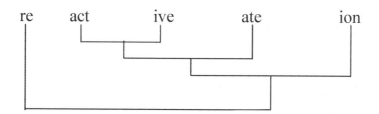

We may express it this way too, using the **branching diagram**:

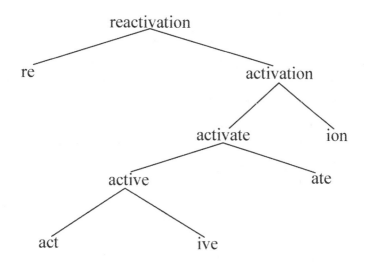

These different diagrams show the immediate constituents (ICs) of words. They are similar to the ICs of sentences. They show the ordering of morphemic strata within a word; they show the steps of the word-building process, step by step. They show the layers of the internal structure of the word.

Exercise 2-13

Show the derivational process of these words, using the bracketed diagram here on this page or any other diagram using additional sheets if necessary.

1. lengthened _____
2. relationships _____
3. independently _____
4. conclusions _____
5. impressionism _____
6. postexaminations _____
7. discontinuousness _____
8. hypothesizing _____

Constraints on Derivation

As it is well known, there are constraints at the phonemic level: no phoneme can accept all phonemes after it. For example, English does not have words beginning with *bg, bf, bj,* or *bk.* To add, at the syntactic level, words are not free to occur anywhere. For example, a sequence like **Boy the eating was apples some* is not acceptable nor grammatical.

Similarly, at the morphological level, morphemes are not free to occur anywhere inside the word. For example, sequences like these are not acceptable: **ed+en+length, *al+pose+pre+ion, *place+re+ity+able,* whereas consequences like these are acceptable: *lengthened, prepositional,* and *replaceability.*

To conclude, language, being a system, has its rules and constraints, i.e., restrictions, at all levels: phonemic, morphological, and syntactic.

Blocking

Sometimes a derivational rule is not allowed to function; this is called **blocking**. What are the reasons for this blocking?

1. An existing word may block another, e.g., *thief* blocks **stealer*.

2. Adjectives ending in *-ous* allow nouns ending in *-ness*, not in *-ity*, e.g., *gloriousness, fallaciousness, spaciousness, furiousness*, but not **gloriousity*.

3. Awkwardness may block some adverbs derived from adjectives, e.g., **sillily, *friendlily, *sisterlily*.

4. The semantic factor may cause some blocking. We can say *short-sighted boy*, but not **two-carred family*. This Adj (or numeral)+N_1-*ed*+N_2 pattern requires that N_1 is an inalienable part of N_2.

5. The prefix *un-* is added to the positive pole, not to the negative pole, of an adjective. Thus, *unwell, unloved, unwise, unclean*, and *unhappy* block words like **unill, *unhated, *unfoolish, *undirty*, and **unsad*, respectively.

6. Synonymy may block some derivatives. If a synonym is already there, it may block deriving another synonymous derivative, e.g., *bore, guide, spy*, and *judge* block **borer, *guider, *spier*, and **judger*. If a noun ending in *-ant* is there, it blocks a synonym ending in *-er*, e.g., *applicant, accountant, participant* and *intoxicant* block **applier, *accounter, *participater* and **intoxicater*, respectively.

Families of Derivatives

Derivation makes families of derivatives. Such a family is a group of different derivatives having the same root but with different affixes, e.g., *phone, phonetic, phonetics, phonology, phonemics, phonetician, phonemic, phonological, telephone.* All these words and certainly some more make one family of derivatives because they all have the same root.

Such a group of words is called a **derivational family** or **a derivational paradigm**, which uses derivational suffixes to make words. This term contrasts with the term an **inflectional paradigm**, where only inflectional suffixes are used to make the words of the group, e.g., *write, writes, wrote, written, writing,* or *boy, boys, boy's, boys',* or *large, larger, largest.*

Exercise 2-14

Mention as many derivatives as you can in order to make one family of derivatives. You may use the dictionary here.

1. occur _____
_____
_____

2. receive _____
_____
_____

3. assume _____
_____
_____

4. efficient _____

_____

_____

5. pronounce _____

_____

_____

Derivational Rules

Every derivational case has a derivational rule behind it. Here are some examples:

1. *dictation* = V + *ion* → N
2. *dictator* = V + *er/or* → N
3. *quickly* = Adj + *ly* → Adv
4. *harmless* = N + *less* → Adj
5. *colorful* = N + *ful* → Adj
6. *spoonful* = N + *ful* → N
7. *smoking* = V + *ing* → N
8. *enrich* = *en* + Adj → V
9. *whiten* = Adj + *en* → V
10. *creativity* = Adj + *ity* → N

Some of these rules are **productive rules**: they apply to thousands of bases. For example, Rule 2 allows adding *-er* to the V; almost all verbs submit to this rule. Rule 3 allows adding *-ly* to the Adj, and many adjectives submit to this rule. Rule 7 allows adding *-ing* to the verb, and verbs submit to this rule.

In contrast, some derivational rules are **semi-productive rules:** they only apply to some bases involved.

For example, Rule 8 does not apply to all adjectives: Adjectives such as *good, bad, hot,* and *cold* do not allow *en-* as a prefix to make verbs. The same is true about Rule 9.

Thus, affixes vary in the degree of their **productivity**, depending on their activity in word formation. The more active an affix is, the more productive it is. We can, of course, talk about **prefix productivity**, **infix productivity**, and **suffix productivity.**

Footnotes

1. Exercise 2-5 and Exercise 2-6 are identical in instructions, and the purpose of having them both is providing more practice.

2. The suffix *-ish* sometimes changes N into Adj, e.g., *Polish* and *Danish*, derived from *Pole* and *Dane*, respectively.

3. Nationality-forming suffixes do not change the stem class, e.g., *Japan*→ *Japanese*, *Jordan*→ *Jordanian*, where N has remained N. However, the output word can be used as an Adj as well, e.g., *Japanese food*.

CHAPTER 3

COMPOUNDING

Compounding is a frequent word-formation process, e.g., *chalkboard, football*. Such words are called **compounds** or **compound words**. They can be compound nouns, e.g., *blackboard,* compound adjectives, e.g., *tax-free,* compound prepositions, e.g., *into, onto,* or compound verbs, e.g., *underestimate.*

Compounding is different from deriving. The former is combining two words into one word, e.g., *class+ room→classroom,* whereas deriving is combining a root and one affix or more, e.g., *en+large→enlarge.*

Structure of Compounds

There are at least twelve types of compounds, shown in Table 3-1 below. Study the table carefully so as to have a good idea about compound types.

Table 3-1: Types of Compounds

No.	Derivational Rule	Examples
1.	N + N → N	*tablecloth, classroom, court hall*
2.	N + Adj → Adj	*tax-free, sky blue, watertight*
3.	N + V → V	*breathtaking, hair-raising, homemade* [1]

Table 3-1: Continued

No.	Derivational Rule	Examples
4.	N + Adv → N	*passer-by, looker-on*
5.	Adj + N → N	*greenhouse, blackboard*
6.	Adj + Adj → Adj	*icy-cold, white-hot*
7.	Adj + V → V	*deepfreeze*
8.	V + N → N	*pickpocket, watchdog*
9.	V + V → V	*hearsay, make-believe*
10.	Adv + N → N	*overcoat, underworld*
11.	Adv + Adj → Adj	*evergreen, wide awake*
12.	Adv + V → V	*ill-treat, understand*

Exercise 3-1

Write down the derivational rule of each compound.
Example: *red hot = Adj + Adj → Adj.*

1. outlaw   11. moonlight
2. word order   12. overeat
3. indoors   13. under-achievement
4. outdoors   14. over-employment
5. workbook   15. credit hour
6. copybook   16. evening studies
7. exercise book   17. aftermath
8. volley ball   18. easy-going
9. breakfast   19. good-looking
10. daytime   20. handmade

Head of the Compound

Every compound usually, but not always, has a head. A *pocket knife* is a *knife*, not a *pocket*, so *knife* is the head of this compound. A *knife pocket* is a *pocket*, not a *knife*, so *pocket* is the head. The compound is usually made of two words, the more important one of which is the **head**. This head is usually the rightmost word of the whole compound.

If you examine the compounds more closely, you find that if the second word, i.e., head, in the compound is a N, the whole compound is usually a N, e.g., *pocket dictionary*. If the head is a V, the compound is usually a V, e.g., *hearsay*. If the head is an Adj, the compound is usually an Adj, e.g., *red-hot*.

Although most compounds have heads and thus called **headed compounds**, some compounds do not have heads and thus called **headless compounds**. For example, a *greenhouse* is not a *house*, a *turncoat* (= a *traitor*) is not a *coat*. Such compounds are called **exocentric compounds**. In contrast, headed compounds are called **endocentric compounds**, e.g., *football*.

Concerning the head position, most compounds are right-headed, i.e., having the head on the **right-hand** of the compound, e.g., *pocket knife*. This is called the **right-hand head rule** (RHR). However, some compounds are **left-headed**, e.g., *passer-by, father-in-law*.

Exercise 3-2

What is the head of each compound? What is the class of the head (N, V, Adj, Adv)? What is the class of the whole compound?

No.	Compound	Head of the Compound	Class of the Head	Class of the Compound
1.	cornflakes	flakes	N	N
2.	high school			
3.	sleepwalk			

No.	Compound	Head of the Compound	Class of the Head	Class of the Compound
4.	afterthought			
5.	lifelong			
6.	bittersweet			
7.	spoonfeed			
8.	classmate			
9.	brainwash			
10.	daydream			

Writing Compounds

There are three ways to write compounds:

1. A compound written as a single word, e.g., *thirteen, seventeen, blackboard, classroom.* These compounds are written as one unit, with no space or hyphen in between the two components of the compound. We may call such a compound a **united compound**.

2. A compound written as separate words, i.e., with a space in between, e.g., *swimming suit, evening program, graduate studies, open university, air raid, racial discrimination.* We may call such a compound a **spaced compound**.

3. A compound written with hyphenation, e.g., *icy-cold, red-hot, to-night, easy-going.* We may call such a compound a **hyphenated compound**.

It seems that a compound in its early usage is written as separate words. As usage becomes more and more frequent, the two words get closer and closer, and a hyphen is then used. When the compound later becomes very frequent, the hyphen disappears, and the two words are written as a single word.

English, however, does not treat compounds consistently as to how they are written. Words such as *twenty-five*, for example, are sometimes written as a single word, i.e., *twentyfive*. In contrast, *teen* numbers from 13 to 19 are always written as single words, e.g., *sixteen*, probably due to their very frequent usage. Words like *to-morrow* and *to-day*, once hyphenated, are now no longer written with a hyphen; they are written as united compounds, e.g., *today*.

Exercise 3-3

Decide how each compound should be written: one single word (1W), with a hyphen (H), or two separate words (S). You can consult the dictionary. Each compound will appear here as two separate words only tentatively.

1. high born	_____	**7.** rain bow	_____
2. sleep walk	_____	**8.** master key	_____
3. chalk board	_____	**9.** master piece	_____
4. to night	_____	**10.** air port	_____
5. yester day	_____	**11.** safety belt	_____
6. twenty three	_____	**12.** swimming pool	_____

Compounds within Compounds

Sometimes a compound is used as the first component within a larger compound, e.g., *four-year plan*. Here *four-year* is a compound, which is used inside the larger compound. We may call this process **complex compounding** or **recursive compounding**, i.e., repeated compounding. Another example is *dog food box*, where *dog food* is a compound making the first element of the larger compound.

Exercise 3-4

Identify the first component and the second component of each compound.

1. London street guide	London	street guide
2. police patrol car	————	————
3. stock market report	————	————
4. electric wire factory	————	————
5. modern language department	————	————
6. hard cover books	————	————
7. social science magazine	————	————
8. Amman road network	————	————

Compounds or Phrases?

Look at these items:

1. *the Whíte Hòuse*
2. *the whìte hóuse*
3. *bláckbòard*
4. *blàck bóard*
5. *gréenhòuse*
6. *greèn hóuse*
7. *drópkìcked*
8. *róad màp*
9. *fóx hùnter*

How can we distinguish a compound from a normal noun phrase? To answer this question, there are four tests:

1. The first test is the **stress test**, which works best in the case of N-N or Adj-N compounds. In such compounds, we often stress the first word, but in phrases we usually stress the second word. In the above list, units 1, 3, 5, 7, 8, and 9 are compounds, but units 2, 4, and 6 are phrases, i.e., non-compounds. The meaning, of course, is different. For example, a *bláckbòard* is different from a *blàck bóard*. The first one is a *chalkboard,* but the second is a *board that is black.* For stress symbols, see Appendix III.

2. The second test is the **tense test**. If a word is a verb compound, the tense suffix is taken by the second word, not the first, e.g., *dropkicked,* not **droppedkick.*

3. The third test is the **plural test**. In noun compounds, the second element is the one that takes the plural suffix, e.g., *fox hunters,* not **foxes hunter, road maps* not **roads map.* The exception is left-headed compounds, e.g., *passersby.*

4. The fourth test is the ***very* test**, especially with Adj-N units. A compound of the Adj-N type does not accept *very,* e.g., **very blackboard, *very greenhouse.* In contrast, an Adj-N phrase accepts *very* if the Adj is gradable, e.g., *a very green house, a very black board.*

Exercise 3-5

Which of these is a compound (C) and which is a non-compound (NC)? Why?

1. sugarcoat _____   **8.** abroad _____
2. coated with sugar _____   **9.** warship _____
3. airplane _____   **10.** daydreaming _____
4. plane in the air _____   **11.** infrared _____
5. clear example _____   **12.** ultraviolet _____
6. sweet potatoes _____   **13.** supersonic _____
7. fireworks _____   **14.** into _____

Types of Compounds

The relation between the compound and its meaning is not always the same. For example, a *policeman* is a *man,* a *warship* is a *ship*, an *airplane* is a *plane*, a *pocket knife* is a *knife*. Such compounds are called **endocentric compounds**. The meaning of each compound is directly related to the meaning of its component words.

In contrast, a *turncoat* is a *traitor*, not a *coat*. Such words are called **exocentric compounds**; the meaning of each compound is not the total of the meanings of its components. Look at Table 3-2, which shows a list of exocentric compounds.

Table 3-2: Exocentric Compounds

No.	compound	Meaning
1.	turncoat	traitor
2.	greenbottle	a kind of flies
3.	highbrow	well-educated person
4.	bigwig	prestigious person
5.	egghead	a man of wide knowledge

Most compounds consist of two words, and a few of them consist of three words, e.g., *father-in-law*. Of course, most compounds are endocentric, and a few of them are exocentric.

Exercise 3-6

Which compound is endocentric (EN), and which one is exocentric (EX)?

1. redcoat _____   5. waterproof _____
2. steamship _____   6. word meaning _____
3. blue collar _____ 7. white collar _____
4. landlord _____   8. sunshine

Another area that requires examination is the *-ing* compound, where the first component ends in *-ing*, e.g., *looking glass*. A *jumping bean* jumps, a *falling star* falls, but a *looking glass* does not look, nor does *laughing gas* laugh.

On the surface, a *looking glass* is structurally similar to a *falling star*, but at the deep structure level, they are not. In the former, the *glass* is used for *looking*, but in the latter the *star* is not used for *falling*. In the former, the *glass* does not look, but in the latter, the *star* does fall. The reason for this difference is that *looking* is a verbal noun, but *falling* is a participial adjective. For a summary of the types of compounds, see Figure 3-1.

Exercise 3-7
Which *-ing* form is used adjectivally (Adj), and which is used nominally (N), i.e., as a noun?

1. walking stick _____   6. eating child _____
2. walking child _____   7. jumping stick _____
3. running water _____   8. climbing tools _____
4. adding machine _____   9. climbing plant _____
5. eating apple _____   10. thinking time _____

Paraphrasing Compounds
Compounds can be paraphrased in different ways, depending on the internal structure of each compound. Look at these compounds and their paraphrases.

1. *sunrise*   : *the rise of the sun*
2. *hangman*   : *the man who hangs*
3. *brainwashing*   : *washing the brain*
4. *chewing gum*   : *gum for chewing*
5. *sun-bathing*   : *bathing in the sun*

6. *handwriting*   : *writing with the hand*
7. *oil well*   : *a well producing oil*
8. *fire engine*   : *an engine against fire*
9. *glass window*   : *a window made of glass*
10. *frogman*   : *a man like a frog*
11. *coffee time*   : *time for coffee*
12. *breath-taking*   : *that takes breath*
13. *new-laid*   : *laid newly*
14. *easy-going*   : *going easily*
15. *sea-green*   : *green like the sea*
16. *deaf-mute*   : *deaf and mute*
17. *baby-sit*   : *sit with the baby*

Although all the seventeen examples above are compounds, each one of them is obviously structured in a unique way. The evidence to this comes from the fact that each compound is paraphrased differently. In other words, the deep structure of each compound may be or is, in fact, different from the deep structures of the other compounds.

Exercise 3-8

Paraphrase each of these compounds in a way similar to one of the seventeen paraphrases given in the previous section.

1. earthquake _____   7. tear gas _____
2. washing machine _____ 8. oak tree _____
3. songwriter _____   9. heart-breaking _____
4. cooking apple _____   10. self-employed _____
5. typing paper _____   11. bitter-sweet _____
6. gunfight _____   12. lip-read _____

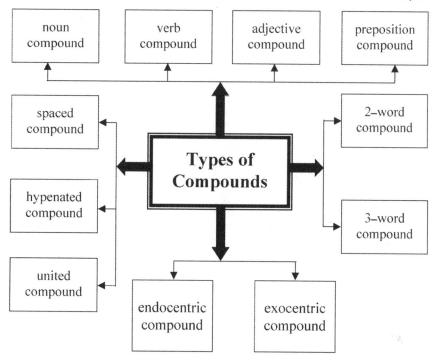

Figure 3-1: Types of Compounds

Noun Compounds

Compounds can be classified into four main classes: noun compounds, adjective compounds, verb compounds, and preposition compounds.[2] Let us, first, see how noun compounds are internally structured. Such compounds are structured in these ways:

A. Subject and verb compounds: When paraphrased, such compounds can be expressed by a subject-V structure, e.g., *washing machine→ the machine washes.*

1. N + Deverbal N, e.g., *earthquake, headache*. A deverbal N is a noun derived from a verb and has the same form of the verb, e.g., *walk, talk, set*.

2. V + N, e.g., *flashlight, hangman*

3. Verbal N + N, e.g., *washing machine*, where a verbal noun is a noun derived by adding *-ing* to the verb. Some grammarians call it a gerund.

B. Verb and object compounds: If you paraphrase such compounds, the paraphrase reveals a V-object structure, e.g., *storytelling→ telling a story.*

1. N + Verbal N, e.g., *story-telling, brainwashing*

2. N + agentive N, e.g., *glass-cleaner, novel-writer*. An agentive N is a noun ending with *-er*.

3. N + Deverbal N, e.g., *birth-control, book review*

4. V + N, e.g., *pickpocket*

5. Verbal N + N, e.g., *chewing gum*

C. Verb and adverbial compounds: The paraphrase of such compounds reveals a V-Adv structure, e.g., *adding machine→ machine for adding.*

1. Verbal N + N, e.g., *adding machine*

2. N + Verbal N, e.g., *sun-bathing*

3. N + Agentive N, e.g., *baby-sitter*

4. N + Deverbal N, e.g., *homework*

5. V + N, e.g., *searchlight*

D. Verbless compounds: The surface structures of these noun compounds do not include any verbs. However, their deep structures show a variety of semantic relations as in Examples 1-5: *moved by, producing, having, quality,* and *like*, respectively.

1. N + N, e.g., *windmill*

   2. N + N, e.g., *toy factory*
   3. N + N, e.g., *doorknob*
   4. Adj + N, e.g., *hard cover*
   5. N + N, e.g., *frogman*

Adjective Compounds

Some compounds are adjectives. Internally, they are structured in different ways:

A. Verb and object compounds: The paraphrase of such compounds reveals a V-Object structure, e.g., *heart-breaking* → *breaking the heart*.

N + *-ing* participle, e.g. *breath-taking*

B. Verb and Adverbial compounds: The paraphrase of these compounds reveals a V-Adv structure, e.g., *easy-going* → *going easily*.

   1. N + *-ing* participle, e.g., *mouth-watering*
   2. N + *-ed* participle, e.g., *handmade*
   3. Adj + *-ing* participle, e.g., *easy-going*
   4. Adj + *-ed* participle, e.g., *new-laid*

C. Verbless compounds: These compounds do not have verbs neither in their surface structure nor in their deep structure.

   1. N + Adj, e.g., *homesick*   (*with regard to*)
   2. N + Adj, e.g., *brick-red*   (*like*)
   3. Adj + Adj, e.g., *deaf-blind*   (*and*)

Verb Compounds

Some compounds are verbs:
   1. N + V, e.g., *sightsee*   (*object*)
   2. N + V, e.g., *babysit*   (*with*)

Exercise 3-9

What is the class of each compound: N, Adj, or V?

1. firing squad _____   6. bloodtest _____
2. dressmaking _____   7. lab-technician _____
3. daydream _____   8. lip-read _____
4. grass-green _____   9. quick-frozen _____
5. good-looking _____   10. self-taught _____

Exercise 3-10

What is the internal structure of each compound?
Example: self-teaching = N + *-ing* participle.

1. brainstorming _____   7. seashore _____
2. sea waves _____   8. handmade _____
3. drilling machine _____   9. homework _____
4. gate guard _____   10. babysitter _____
5. self-rule _____   11. apple tree _____
6. white-wash _____   12. rose-red _____

Footnotes

1. The compound here is a N plus a present participle or a past participle, and these two participles are verb forms. The output is a verb in form, but adjectival in function or usage.

2. Because preposition compounds such as *into* and *onto* are very limited in number, they will not be emphasized in our discussion of compounds in this chapter.

CHAPTER 4

INFLECTION

Another major way of making words is inflection. This inflection is realized by adding an inflectional suffix to the stem. This stem can be one of these classes: noun, verb, adjective, e.g., *chair+s, learn+ed, large+est.*

Inflectional Suffixes

English has eight inflectional suffixes: two with nouns, four with verbs, and two with adjectives. These are the eight suffixes:

1. The plural suffix or the plural morpheme, symbolized as $\{-S_1\}$, e.g., *watches, streets, rooms.* In spelling, it is either <-es> or <s>, e.g., church+*es*, car+*s*. In pronunciation, it is either /ɨz/ after sibilants, /s/ after voiceless sounds, or /z/ after voiced sounds, e.g., *bus+/ɨz/, book+/s/, door+/z/.* These three are allomorphs of $\{-S_1\}$.

2. The possessive suffix, symbolized as $\{-S_2\}$. In spelling, it is either ' or 's, e.g., *the boys' books, the boy's books.* In pronunciation, there are four varieties:/ɨz/, /s/, /z/, and /Ø/, i.e., zero, e.g., *George+/ɨz/, Dick+/s/, John+/z/,*

71

Jesus+/Ø/, respectively, spelled as *George's, Dick's, John's,* and *Jesus'*. These four are called the allomorphs of {-S₂}.

3. The present-simple suffix, symbolized as {-S₃}. In spelling, it is either <es> or <s>, e.g., *go+es, speak+s*. In pronunciation, it is /ɨz/, /s/, /z/, e.g., *wash+/ɨz/, speak+/s/, learn+/z/*. These three varieties are called the **allomorphs** of the present-simple morpheme.

4. The past suffix or the past morpheme, symbolized as {-D₁}, e.g., *hesitated*. In regular spelling, it is <ed>, e.g., *want+ed, learn+ed, call+ed*. In pronunciation, it is either /ɨd/, /t/, or /d/ as in *wanted, passed,* and *cleaned,* respectively. These three are allomorphs of {D₁}.

5. The past participle suffix, symbolized as {-D₂}, e.g., *cleaned*. In regular spelling, it is <ed>. In pronunciation, it is either /ɨd/, /t/, or /d/, identical with {D₁}. These three are allomorphs of {D₂}.

6. The progressive suffix or the present participle suffix or morpheme, symbolized as {-ing}. In spelling, it is always <ing>, and in pronunciation, it is always /-ɨŋ/.

7. The comparative suffix or morpheme, symbolized as {-er} and pronounced /ər/. It is added to an adjective in the positive degree to make the adjective in the comparative degree, e.g., *larger, hotter*.

8. The superlative suffix or morpheme, symbolized as {-est} and pronounced /ɨst/, added to a positive-degree adjective to make a superlative adjective, e.g., *largest, hottest*.

Exercise 4-1

Give the type of the underlined inflectional suffix. Choose one type of the eight types mentioned in the previous section: $\{S_1, S_2, S_3, D_1, D_2, \text{ing}, \text{er}, \text{or est}\}$.

1. scienc<u>es</u>	_____	6. skimm<u>ing</u>	_____
2. explor<u>es</u>	_____	7. pur<u>er</u>	_____
3. advanc<u>ed</u>	_____	8. poor<u>est</u>	_____
4. creat<u>ed</u>	_____	9. experienc<u>ed</u>	_____
5. Ali<u>'s</u>	_____	10. act<u>ing</u>	_____

Exercise 4-2

Decide whether each underlined unit is an inflectional suffix (I), derivational suffix (D), or neither (N).

1.work<u>er</u>	_____	7. wi<u>se</u>	_____
2. strong<u>er</u>	_____	8. str<u>ing</u>	_____
3. New York<u>er</u>	_____	9. runn<u>ing</u>	_____
4. w<u>est</u>	_____	10. three m<u>'s</u>	_____
5. fin<u>est</u>	_____	11. Dick<u>'s</u> bag	_____
6. win<u>s</u>	_____	12. stick<u>s</u>	_____

Notice that each of the plural suffix and the possessive one is added to a noun and the output is a noun, with no change in class. The present suffix, the past one, the past participle one, and the progressive one are added to a verb and the output is a verb, with no change in class. The comparative suffix and the superlative suffix are added to the adjective, and the output is also an adjective, with no change in class. All these suffixes appear in Figure 4-1.

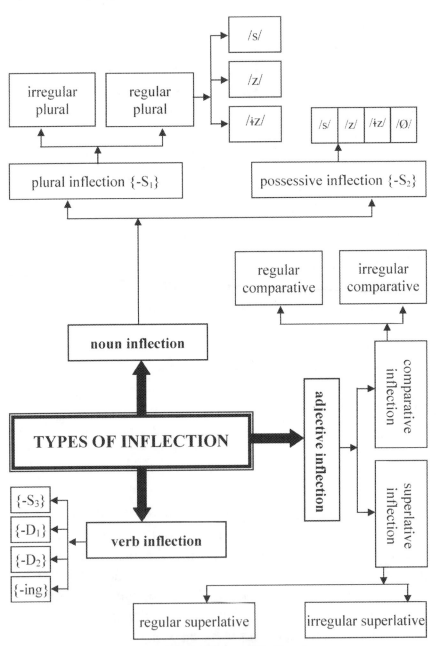

Figure 4-1: Types of Inflection

Inflectional and Derivational Suffixes

Inflectional suffixes differ from derivational suffixes in several ways:

1. As for number in the English language, inflectional suffixes are very few: they are only eight suffixes. In contrast, derivational suffixes are about one hundred.

2. As for class change, inflectional suffixes do not change the class of the stem, e.g., book+*s, go+ing, weak+er*. The N remains a N, the Adj remains an Adj, and the V remains a V. In contrast, derivational suffixes often, but not always, cause a class change, e.g., *simple→simplify* (Adj→V), *weak→weakness* (Adj→N), *child→childish* (N→Adj). In fact, derivational suffixes are three types concerning class change:

a. Suffixes that change the base class, e.g., *hard+ship* (Adj→N), black+*en* (Adj→V), *courage+ous* (N→Adj).

b. Suffixes that do not change the base class, e.g., *hero+ine, host+ess.*

c. Suffixes that keep the base class, but change the sub-class, e.g., *friend+ship* (common N→abstract N), *psychology+ist* (abstract N→common N).

In contrast, inflectional suffixes never cause any change in the class or sub-class of the base.

3. As for the number of suffixes in one word, a word cannot take more than one inflectional suffix, i.e., one of these at a time: {S_1, S_2, S_3, D_1, D_2, -ing, -er, -est}. A word like **learn+ed+ing* or **weak+er+est* is impossible. The only exception is S_1 and S_2: a plural noun can take the possessive suffix in the zero variety, e.g., *the boys' bags*. However, no realized $\{S_1\}$, i.e., not zero, can take a realized $\{S_2\}$, i.e., not zero. In other words, a word like *boys* cannot accept *'s* after it. Thus, in this latter sense no word can take two inflectional suffixes. In contrast, a word may take three derivational suffixes, e.g., *inter+nation+al+ize+ion (=internationalization), globe+al+ize+ion (=globalization)*.

4. As for order, inflectional suffixes come after derivational ones, e.g., *probable+ity+s (=probabilities), ideal+ize+ing*. After the derivational suffix, you may add a derivational suffix, e.g., *plural+ize+ion(=pluralization)*, or an inflectional suffix, e.g., *in+flect+ion+s (=inflections)*. In contrast, after the inflectional suffix, you cannot add any suffix, e.g., *book+s*, with the exception of the possessive zero suffix after the plural suffix, e.g., *boys'*.

5. As for closing the word, an inflectional suffix closes the word since it does not allow any other suffix to follow it, whereas the derivational suffix may allow other suffixes, whether derivational or inflectional, to follow, e.g., *origin+al+ity*, where *-al* allows *-ity* to follow.

6. As for productivity, inflectional suffixes are more productive than derivational suffixes. For example, $\{S_3\}$, i.e., the present morpheme, goes with almost all present verbs having a third-person singular subject, and $\{-ing\}$ goes with all lexical verbs.[1] In contrast, the derivational suffix *-ize* is taken by only a limited number of adjectives, e.g., *modernize*.

7. As for affecting the meaning of the stem or base, inflectional suffixes do not change the referential meaning or cognitive meaning of the base. For example, *book* and *books* have the same referential meaning; the only difference is in the number of books; *sleep* and *slept* have the same referential meaning with the only difference in tense, and so on with the other inflectional suffixes. In contrast, derivational suffixes change the meaning considerably, e.g., *learn/learner, real/realize*.

Exercise 4-3

Write down the inflectional suffix in its graphic form and phonemic form, and mention its type ({S_1, S_2, S_3, D_1, D_2, ing, er, est}).

No.	Word	Inflectional Suffix Graphically	Inflectional Suffix Phonemically	Suffix Type Symbolically
1.	doors	\<s\>	/z/	{-S_1}
2.	opens			
3.	explained			
4.	earlier			
5.	kicking			
6.	John's			
7.	simplest			
8.	looked			

Suffixal Homophones

Pairs of words like *sun/son, I/eye,* and *sea/see* are called **homophones**, because they are pronounced in the same way although they have different meanings and spellings. Similarly, there are suffixes that are pronounced in the same way and have different meanings. They are called **homophonous suffixes** or **suffixal homophones**. Let us look at these groups.

A. The {-er} group. This group contains four suffixal homophones of {-er}:

1. Comparative {-er}. It is the inflectional {-er}, i.e., the comparative {-er}, added to the positive Adj to make a comparative Adj, e.g., *colder, hotter, larger, smaller.*

2. Agentive {-er}. It is added to the V to make an agentive noun, e.g., *teacher, worker, learner, runner.* This {-er} is derivational, not inflectional.

3. Repetitive {-er}. It conveys the meaning of repetition, e.g., *chatter, mutter, flicker, glitter.* This {-er} is derivational, not inflectional.

4. Relational {-er}. This is added to nouns to make nouns. You can call it a N-to-N suffix, e.g., *teenager, teener, Londoner*, meaning *related to.* This {-er} is derivational, not inflectional.

Exercise 4-4

What type of {-er} is at the end of each word: comparative (C), agentive (A), repetitive (R1), or relational (R2)?

1. singer	_____	6. chatter	_____
2. bigger	_____	7. miner	_____
3. wider	_____	8. forty-niner	_____
4. New Yorker	_____	9. seller	_____
5. reminder	_____	10. glitter	_____

B. The {-ing} group. This group includes three different suffixal homophones of {-ing}:

1. Verbal {-ing}. This inflectional -*ing* is added to the V base and functions verbally, e.g., *a running horse, a burning house*, i.e., *a horse that is running, a house that is burning*. This -*ing* can also be called the **progressive -*ing***, e.g., *He is working hard.*

2. Nominal {-ing}. The produced word here, often called a gerund or verbal noun, is used as a noun, not as a V, e.g., *meeting*. Such a word may sometimes allow pluralization, e.g., *meetings*, whereas the verbal {-ing} does not allow pluralization, e.g., **speakings*. This -*ing* is derivational, not inflectional.

3. Adjectival {-ing}. The produced word here is used as an Adj, e.g., *an interesting story*. The test here can be the *very* test: the word accepts *very* before it, e.g., *very interesting*, or other intensifiers such as *rather* or *quite*. Another test is accepting *more* or *most*, e.g., *a more interesting story*. A third test is the *seem* test, e.g., *The story seems interesting*. The adjectival derivational -*ing* passes the *very* test, the *more* test, and the *seem* test. In contrast, other -*ing's* do not pass such tests.

Exercise 4-5

Which {-ing} is in each word: N-*ing*, V-*ing*, or Adj-*ing*?
1. **Running** is a good exercise.   _____
2. He is **running** fast.   _____
3. Look at this **charming** sight.   _____
4. They are **meeting** next week.   _____
5. The **meeting** was successful.   _____
6. I agree to this old **saying**.   _____

7. He is **telling** the truth.   _____

8. This **drawing** is expensive.   _____

9. He is **drawing** beautiful pictures.   _____

10. **Sleeping** too much is not healthy.   _____

C. The {-ed} group. This group includes three homophonous suffixes:

1. Past {-ed}. This is the {D_1} inflectional suffix, added to the base (or stem) of the verb to make the past form, e.g., *learned, moved, examined.* Of course, this is a verbal {-ed}.

2. Past participle {-ed}. This is the {D_2} inflectional suffix, added to the base verb to make the past participle, e.g., *learned, moved, examined,* each of which has either {D_1} or {D_2}, distinguishable through the context. For example, *moved* in *He moved yesterday* has {D_1}, but *moved* in *He has moved* has {D_2}.

3. Adjectival {-ed}. The word here accepts qualifiers like *more, most, very, rather,* or *quite,* whereas the verbal {-ed} does not accept such words. For example, *interested* in *He was interested in the subject* is adjectival, not verbal.

Exercise 4-6

Does the bold-typed word have a past {-ed} (P), past participle {-ed} (PP), or adjectival {-ed} (Adj)?

1. He has **printed** a lot of materials.   _____

2. He was a **neglected** child.   _____

3. This question is rather **complicated**.   _____

4. His **preferred** book was lost.   _____

5. His car was **stolen**.   _____

6. He has **invited** all his friends.   _____

7. He has two **reserved** seats.   _____

8. He was a **reserved** man.   _____
9. He was **excited** at the film.   _____
10. He became **worried** about his brother.   _____

Regular and Irregular Inflection

Derivational suffixes do not show irregular affixational cases, whereas inflectional suffixes are in most cases regular but in some cases irregular. Such irregular inflections especially appear in the plurality morpheme $\{-S_1\}$, the past morpheme $\{-D_1\}$, the past participle morpheme $\{-D_2\}$, the comparative morpheme $\{-er\}$, and the superlative morpheme $\{-est\}$. Even $\{-S_3\}$, the present suffix, shows a few cases of irregularity, e.g., $be+\{-S_3\} \rightarrow is$, $have+\{-S_3\} \rightarrow has$.

Therefore, almost all inflectional suffixes show some irregular forms. The only inflectional suffix that is always regular is the $\{-ing\}$ morpheme, taken by all lexical verbs, e.g., *going, writing, sitting*. Of course, auxiliary verbs that are modals do not take $\{-ing\}$, e.g., *can, must, may, will, shall, could*. However, primary auxiliaries take $\{-ing\}$, i.e., *having, being,* and *doing*.

Irregular verbs take infixes instead of suffixes, e.g., $took \rightarrow take+/ey \rightarrow u/$, $spoke \rightarrow speak+/iy \rightarrow ow/$, $lay \rightarrow lie+/ay \rightarrow ey/$, $know \rightarrow knew+/ow \rightarrow uw/$. With irregular plurals, a similar change may happen: $feet \rightarrow foot+/u \rightarrow iy/$, $mice \rightarrow mouse+/aw \rightarrow ay/$. For the symbols of English phonemes, see Appendix III.

With some irregular verbs, a zero allomorph may be added, e.g., $cut \rightarrow cut, cut, put \rightarrow put, put$, $broadcast \rightarrow broadcast$, *broadcast*, examples of zero allomorphs of $\{-D_1\}$ and $\{-D_2\}$.

With a few cases of irregular nouns, a zero allomorph may be added too, e.g., *deer→deer, sheep→sheep, fish→fish,* examples of a **zero plural allomorph**.

In very few cases, the whole form may change, e.g., *go→went,* which shows no suffixation or infixation; it is a complete change of the base. Such a case is called **suppletion**.

Exercise 4-7

Are the bold-typed words examples of regular (R) or irregular (I) inflection?

1. These **criteria** are quite clear. _____
2. The **worst** part is to come. _____
3. Do your **best**. _____
4. It will be **proved** later. _____
5. The computer is rich of **data**. _____
6. He **has** a lot to tell. _____
7. They **are** here now. _____
8. He **might** be there. _____
9. She needs blood **analyses**. _____
10. **Elephants** can be harmful. _____

Notice that irregular inflection, especially with nouns and verbs, often uses a **replacive allomorph**, usually but inaccurately called an infix. Such inflections can be expressed this way:

sang = *sing* + /i→æ/
spoke = *speak* + /iy→ow/
feet = *foot* + /u→iy/
mice = *mouse* + /aw→ay/

Other irregular inflections may use special suffixes, with or without a base change. Here are some examples:

cut	= *cut* + /Ø/
sheep	= *sheep* + /Ø/
slept	= /slep/ + /t/
oxen	= *ox* + /ən/
children	= /čildr/ + /ən/

One may notice that the **irregular inflectional rule** may be **obligatory** or **optional**. Examples of the obligatory rule are *foot/feet, tooth/teeth, sing/sang, sting/stung*. In some cases, the rule is optional. For example, *brother* can be *brothers* or *brethren*; *fish, fishes* or *fish; abide, abided* or *abode; bless, blessed* or *blest; blend, blended* or *blent; broadcast, broadcasted* or *broadcast; dream, dreamed* or *dreamt; light, lighted* or *lit; syllabus, syllabuses* or *syllabi; formula, formulas* or *formulae*. However, in most cases, the irregular inflectional rule is obligatory, and it is optional only in a limited number of cases.

Inflection and Memory

Research has shown that if the inflection of a word is regular, e.g., *car→cars, move→moved*, word frequency has no effect on the **response time** when the plural of a noun or the past form of a verb is asked about. In contrast, if inflection is not regular, the **frequency of usage** correlates negatively with the response time.

In other words, if an irregular plural or past is asked about and it is frequent, the response time becomes shorter in comparison with an irregular but infrequent word. For example, the time response to the past of *cut* is much shorter than that to the past of *string* or *stride*. Thus, the more frequent an irregular form is, the shorter the time of retrieval is. The correlation between frequency and retrieval time is obviously negative.

Inflection and Class

Inflectional suffixes can easily reveal the class of the word. If a word has taken or can take $\{-D_1\}$, $\{-D_2\}$, $\{-ing\}$, or $\{-S_3\}$, then it is a verb. If it has taken or can take $\{-er\}$ or $\{-est\}$, then it is an adjective. If a word has taken or can take $\{-S_1\}$ or $\{-S_2\}$, then it is a noun. Examples of N, V and Adj are *John, go,* and *large,* respectively.

Similarly, derivational suffixes can also mark the class of the word. For example, *-ify, -ize,* and *-en* mark verbs, e.g., *purify, realize, widen.* Suffixes like *-ness, -ment, -ist,* and *-ance* mark nouns, e.g., *largeness, movement, botanist,* and *importance.* Suffixes like *-ish, -ical, -ous, -like,* and *-able* mark adjectives, e.g., *boyish, historical, courageous, childlike, honorable.*

Exercise 4-8

Identify the last suffix of each word, decide whether it is inflectional (I) or derivational (D), and determine the class it marks.

No	Word	Last Suffix	Inflectional or Derivational	Class
1.	elements	-s	I	N
2.	determiner			
3.	similarity			

No	Word	Last Suffix	Inflectional or Derivational	Class
4.	prettier			
5.	visitor			
6.	actress			
7.	glorious			
8.	clearness			
9.	simplify			
10.	meaning			
11.	possible			
12.	occurred			

Footnotes

1. All lexical verbs take -*ing*, not to forget that some verbs cannot take the progressive aspect, e.g., *remember, understand*. However, such non-progressive verbs take the nominal -*ing* to form gerunds, e.g., *understanding*, and can be used in participial clauses as well, e.g., *Understanding the reasons, he managed to solve the problem.*

CHAPTER 5

WORD FORMATION

How are English words formed? There are twelve ways to form words in English: inflection, derivation, compounding, conversion, clipping, blending, backformation, acronymy, onomatopoeia, coinage or invention, reduplication, and antonomasia, not to forget borrowing words from foreign languages, a process gone through by all languages, resulting in words called **borrowings** or **loan words**. In this chapter, we shall discuss these twelve ways one by one.

Inflection

Inflection has been discussed in detail in Chapter 4. To summarize, inflection allows us to form these words:

1. Plural nouns. If the plural affix is added to the singular base, the output will be the plural form, whether regular like *pens, chairs, cats* or irregular like *mice, feet, men.*

2. Past verbs or **forms**. If the past affix is added to the base verb, the output is the past form of the verb, whether regular like *learned, explained, tested,* or irregular like *swam, spoke, knew.*

3. Past participle verbs or forms. By adding the past participle affix to the base verb, the output is the past participle form, whether regular like *added, calculated, relaxed*, or irregular like *begun, spoken, known*.

4. Present participle verbs or forms. By adding {-ing}, i.e., the progressive morpheme or the present participle suffix, to the base verb, the output is the present participle form of the verb, e.g., *speaking, reading*, and *writing*.

5. Present third-person form of the verb. By adding {-S_3} to the base verb, the output is verbs like *goes, speaks, reads*, used with third-person singular subjects like *he, she, it*.

6. Comparative adjectives. By adding {-er} to some adjectives in the positive degree, the output is the comparative adjective, often regular like *louder, lower, softer*, but sometimes irregular like *better, worse, farther*. Of course, not all adjectives accept {-er}; more discussion about this point will appear in later chapters.

7. Superlative adjectives. By adding {-est} to some adjectives in the positive degree, the superlative adjective is obtained whether regular like *loudest, lowest, softest* or irregular like *best, worst, farthest*.

Exercise 5-1

Give the plural forms of these singular nouns.

1. sheep   _____ **8.** formula   _____
2. syllabus   _____ **9.** basis   _____

3. datum	_____	**10.** criterion	_____
4. curriculum	_____	**11.** thesis	_____
5. house	_____	**12.** analysis	_____
6. knife	_____	**13.** stimulus	_____
7. goose	_____	**14.** ox	_____

Exercise 5-2

Give the past, past participle, and present participle of these irregular verbs.

No.	Verb Base	Past	Past Participle	Present Participle
1.	arise			
2.	become			
3.	begin			
4.	bet			
5.	bind			
6.	blow			
7.	breed			
8.	broadcast			
9.	burst			
10.	cling			
11.	dig			
12.	drive			
13.	flee			
14.	forgive			

Exercise 5-3

Give the comparative and superlative inflectional forms of these adjectives if possible.

1. cold   _____   _____
2. hot   _____   _____

3. good   _____   _____
4. bad   _____   _____
5. happy   _____   _____
6. narrow   _____   _____
7. simple   _____   _____
8. mature   _____   _____
9. wonderful   _____   _____
10. attributive _____   _____

Derivation

Details about derivation have been given in Chapter 2. To summarize, new words can be formed by adding prefixes, suffixes, or both to a root or stem. Here is a list of possible derivations related to prefixation:

1. Words with **negative prefixes**, e.g., _unrecommended_, _non-smoker_, _incomplete_, _distrust_, _atheist_

2. Words with **reversative prefixes**, e.g., _decelerate_

3. Words with **pejorative prefixes**, e.g., _misinform_, _maltreatment_

4. Words with **degree prefixes**, e.g., _superimpose_, _outnumber_, _subway_, _minimarket_

5. Words with **attitude prefixes**, e.g., _co-author_, _counteract_, _pro-Chinese_, _anti-socialist_

6. Words with **locative prefixes**, e.g., _super-layer_, _infra-layer_, _intercellular_, _intracellular_

7. Words with **time prefixes**, e.g., _foresee_, _preface_, _post-exam_, _ex-king_, _re-do_

8. Words with **number prefixes**, e.g., _mono-cycle_, _bicycle_, _tricycle_, _rectangle_, _pentagon_

Exercise 5-4

Give the meaning of the bold-typed prefix in each word, and show its function. Example: _unlikely_, Adj→Adj, i.e., added to an Adj to give an Adj.

No.	Word	Prefix Meaning	Prefix Function
1.	**post**-peace	after	N → N
2.	**anti**-freeze		
3.	**con**dense		
4.	**pro**gress		
5.	**semi**-active		
6.	**sub**marine		
7.	**in**credible		
8.	**para**phrase		
9.	**il**legal		
10.	**deca**meter		
11.	**hyper**active		
12.	**trans**late		
13.	**poly**theist		
14.	**ex**-minister		
15.	**en**large		
16.	**be**friend		

Derivation is also obtained by adding one suffix or more to the root or one suffix at a time to the stem. Such derivations may follow one of these processes as examples:

1. N→N derivation. Here, the suffix is added to a noun to make a noun. Examples are _engineer_ (=profession), _booklet_ (=small), _kitchenette_ (=small), _lioness_ (=female), _auntie_ (=dear), _boyhood_ (=status), _princedom_ (=domain), _refinery_ (=place), _slavery_ (=behavior), _machinery_ (=group), _spoonful_ (=amount). Notice that the words between brackets indicate the meanings of the suffixes.

2.   N →N/Adj derivation. Here, a suffix is added to a noun to give a word that is both a N and an Adj. Examples are *Sunnaite*, (=member), *Italian* (=pertaining to), *Japanese* (=nationality or language).

3.   N→V derivation. Here, the suffix is added to a N to make a V. Examples are *theorize* (=make), glorify (=make).

4.   N→Adj derivation. Here, the suffix changes the N into an Adj, e.g., *helpful* (=giving), *helpless* (=without), *yearly* (=related to), *childlike* (=similar), *rainy* (=having), *childish* (=having the character of), *courageous* (=having), *heroic* (=related to), *musical* (=related to).

5.   N→Adv derivation. Here, the suffix changes a N into an Adv, e.g., *clockwise* (=in the manner of), *economywise* (=concerning), *eastward(s)* (=in the direction of).

6.   V→N derivation. Here, a suffix is added to a verb to make a noun. Examples are *visitor* (=agent), *inhabitant* (=agent), *employee* (=passive), *dictation* (=action), *amazement* (=action), *refusal* (=action), *smoking* (=action), *drainage* (=activity).

7.   V→Adj derivation. Here, the suffix changes the V into an Adj, e.g. *readable* (=can be, worth to be), *attractive* (=doing).

8.   Adj→N derivation. Here, the suffix is added to change an Adj to a N. Examples are *whiteness* (=state), *equality* (=state).

9.   Adj→V derivation. Here, the suffix changes the Adj into a V, e.g., *purify* (=make), *realize* (=make), *whiten* (=make).

10. Adj→Adv derivation. Here, the suffix changes an Adj into an Adv, e.g., *angri<u>ly</u>* (=in the manner of).

11. Adv→Adv derivation. Here, the suffix is added to an Adv, causing no class change, e.g., *back<u>ward(s)</u>* (=in the direction of).

Exercise 5-5

What is the type of word formation in each case, according to the last suffix: inflection (I) or derivation (D)?

1. editorial	_____	**8.** popularity	_____
2. editor	_____	**9.** gradable	_____
3. editors	_____	**10.** graded	_____
4. editing	_____	**11.** poorer	_____
5. edits	_____	**12.** personal	_____
6. relation	_____	**13.** manhood	_____
7. relationship	_____	**14.** purest	_____

Exercise 5-6

What kind of derivation does each word show: N→N, N→Adj, etc?

1. virtuous	_____	**9.** bracelet	_____
2. downward	_____	**10.** cigarette	_____
3. learnable	_____	**11.** kingdom	_____
4. criminal	_____	**12.** bakery	_____
5. economical	_____	**13.** simplify	_____
6. theorize	_____	**14.** handful	_____
7. glorify	_____	**15.** careful	_____
8. trainee	_____	**16.** astonishment	_____

Compounding

New words can be formed by inflection, derivation, and compounding, the details of which have been given in Chapter 3. As was mentioned there, compounding can give us N-compounds, Adj-compounds, and V-compounds.

In fact, almost each of N, V, Adj, and Adv can be combined with any of N, V, Adj, or Adv to make a compound, with the exception of Adj-Adv. In other words, N can combine with N, V, Adj, or Adv; V with N, Adj, or Adv; Adj with N, Adj, or V; Adv with N, V, Adj, or Adv. For more details and examples, see Chapter 3.

Compounding is a very productive means of forming words. Most compounds consist of two components only, and a few of them have three components, e.g., *brother-in-law*.

What distinguishes the compound noun from the modifier+N structure is the pattern stress. The compound N takes the ´ ` pattern, i.e., strong stress on the first component and a tertiary stress on the second component, e.g., *greénhoùse*. In contrast, the modifier+N structure takes the ˆ ´ pattern or the ` ´ pattern, e.g., *greên hóuse*. For stress symbols, see Appendix III.

Exercise 5-7

Provide these compound nouns with the proper stresses on the first and second components of each.

1. chalkboard _____   6. fireplace _____
2. blackboard _____   7. fire engine _____
3. classroom _____   8. postman _____
4. roommate _____   9. study room _____
5. classmate _____   10. football _____

Exercise 5-8

What is the difference in meaning between these pairs?

1. a. bláckboàrd
   b. blâck bóard _____

2. a. rácing hòrse
   b. râcing hórse _____

3. a. smóking roòm
   b. smôking roóm _____

4. a. Frénch teàcher
   b. Frênch teácher _____

5. a. hígh schòol
   b. hîgh schóol _____

Conversion

Another way of forming words is conversion, where a word changes its class without adding any affixes to it, e.g., *book* (N), *book* (V). Some linguists call conversion **zero derivation** or **zero affixation**, because nothing is added to the word; nevertheless, it has changed its class and its meaning.

In most cases, the semantic relationship between the two meanings stands clear, e.g., *a ship* (N) and *to ship the cargo* (V), *empty* (Adj) and *to empty the boxes* (V), *winter* (N) and *to winter in Cyprus* (V). In most cases as well, conversion is restricted to mono-morphemic words, e.g., *ship* (N, V), *button* (N, V), *walk* (N, V), *talk* (N, V), *up* (Adv, V), *out* (Adv, V).

Conversion works in several directions of class changes:

1. V → N, e.g., *doubt, laugh, catch, throw*

   2. Adj → N, e.g., *daily newspaper→daily*
   3. N → V, e.g., *corner, coat, skin, brake*
   4. Adj → V, e.g., *calm, empty*
   5. Closed-class word → N, e.g., *a must*
   6. Phrase → N, e.g., *many don't knows*
   7. Affix → N, e.g., *many isms*
   8. Non-count → Count, e.g., *two coffees*
   9. Count → Non-count, e.g., *a language→language*
   10. Proper N → Common N, e.g., *a Shakespeare, a sandwich*
   11. Transitive V → Intransitive V, e.g., *melt*

Exercise 5-9

Use each word twice in two sentences as required, to show the conversion process.

1. walk   (N) _____
            (V) _____
2. retreat (N) _____
            (V) _____
3. mail   (N) _____
            (V) _____
4. dry   (Adj) _____
            (V) _____
5. must   (N) _____
            (V) _____
6. meat   (Count) _____
            (Non-count) _____
7. open   (Adj) _____
            (V) _____
8. melt   (Transitive V) _____
            (Intransitive V) _____

9.up   (Adv)   _____

               (V)   _____

  10.down   (Adv)   _____

               (V)   _____

Conversion presents a directionality problem: Is the N derived from the V or the V from the N? For example, is *chair* (N) from *chair* (V) or vice versa? Which is from which? Semantics comes to help here: Which meaning is more basic determines the direction of the relation. As for *chair*, it is N→V; *head*, N→V; *sleep*, V→N, for example.

Disyllabic words show a certain stress pattern in the case of V→N. The N takes a primary stress on the first syllable, and the V takes a primary stress on the second syllable, e.g., *éxport, expórt, ímport, impórt, súrvey, survéy*. However, in the cases of N→V, there is no stress shift, and stress remains on the first syllable with both the N and the V, e.g., *páttern, ádvocate, léver*.

In conversion, most nouns can be verbs, but only some verbs can be nouns. In other words, **denominal verbs**, i.e., verbs from N's, are much more in number than **deverbal nouns**, i.e., N's from V's.

Clipping

Another way of word formation is clipping, which is the omission of one syllable or more from the word. This omission may be initial, i.e., at the beginning of the word, e.g., *telephone→phone*. The omission may also be final, i.e., at the end of the word, e.g., *photograph→photo*. The omission may be both initial and final, e.g., *influenza→flu*. However, the most frequent type of omission is the final omission, e.g., *laboratory→lab*. The output of clipping is called a **clipped word**.

Other examples of clipping are these words: *television→telly, detective→tec, professor→prof, gymnasium→gym*.

Exercise 5-10

What is the clipped word that is usually made from each of the following words?

1. advertisement	_____	**6.** dormitory	_____
2. mathematics	_____	**7.** examination	_____
3. gasoline	_____	**8.** microphone	_____
4. telephone	_____	**9.** Frederick	_____
5. laboratory	_____	**10.** Albert	_____

Exercise 5-11

What is the original word (or source word) of each one of these clipped words?

1. van	_____	**7.** doc	_____
2. chute	_____	**8.** auto	_____
3. Beth	_____	**9.** burger	_____
4. Tony	_____	**10.** zoo	_____
5. Joe	_____	**11.** fax	_____
6. Phil	_____	**12.** cute	_____

Blending

Another way of word formation is blending, and the resulting word is called a **blend**. Blending is the fusion of two words into one, not by compounding, but by combining the first part of one word with the last part of the other word, e.g., *gasoline+alcohol→gasohol, breakfast+lunch→ brunch*. Of course, the meaning of the blend is a comb- ination of the meanings of the two fused words. Notice that the fused parts are often non-morphemic parts.

Exercise 5-12
Give the blends resulting from fusing these pairs of words.

1.(escala)de + eleva(tor) = _____

2.(trans)fer + res(istor) = _____

3.(smo)ke + fo(g) = _____

4.(medi)cal + (care) = _____

5.(sp)iced + h(am) = _____

6.(mo)tor + ho(tel) = _____

7.(bi)nary + digi(t) = _____

8.(mo)dulator + (dem)odulator = _____

9.(ch)annel + t(unnel) = _____

10.(br)eakfast + l(unch) = _____

Backformation

Another way of word formation is **backformation**, which is omitting an affix, usually a suffix, to make a new word. As it is known, in the process of derivation we add affixes to make new words. Here, in backformation, we do exactly the opposite: We subtract a real or supposed affix to make a new word.

Here are some examples of backformation: *resurr- ection→resurrect, housekeeper→housekeep, enthusiasm→ enthuse, donation→donate, orientation→orient.* These

98

words are the results of omitting affixes, rather than adding affixes. Many words in today's English are made through backformation. The word resulting from such a process is called a **backformation**.

Exercise 5-13

What is the word resulting from each backform-ation process?

1. resurrection   ————   6. self-destruction   ————
2. editor   ————   7. oration   ————
3. word processor   ————   8. intuition   ————
4. laser   ————   9. hawker   ————
5. liaison   ————   10. television   ————

Exercise 5-14

What is the origin (or source word) of each following backformation?

1. housekeep   ————   7. beg   ————
2. typewrite   ————   8. edit   ————
3. escalate   ————   9. administrate   ————
4. emote   ————   10. reluct   ————
5. laze   ————   11. resurrect   ————
6. baby-sit   ————   12. denote   ————

Acronymy

Another way of word formation is **acronymy**, whereby a new word is made from the initials of a group of words, e.g., *MP (military police), NATO (North Atlantic Treaty Organization)*. The resulting word is called an **acronym**. Such words have been frequent these days, especially in the fields of business, science, and military vocabulary.

Such words are pronounced as their spelling requires, i.e., like normal words, e.g., *UNESCO (United Nations Educational, Scientific, and Cultural Organization)*. If it is difficult to pronounce the acronym, especially when it has no vowels, each letter is sounded separately, e.g., *NFL (National Football League)*.

As for writing acronyms, they are usually written in capital letters, e.g., *NATO, MP, NFL, UNESCO*. However, some acronyms are written as normal words, e.g., *laser (=light amplification by stimulated emission of radiation), radar (=radio detecting and ranging)*.

As for formation, an acronym is usually formed from the initials of a group of words, e.g., *LA (Los Angeles)*. However, in some cases, it is formed from the beginning segments of a group of words, i.e., not necessarily the first letter, but from the first two or three letters, e.g., *radar*, where *ra* is from *radio*.

Exercise 5-15
Give the original words of these acronyms, and pronounce them.

1. OK	_____	**10.** SA	_____
2. OPEC	_____	**11.** JD	_____
3. WASP	_____	**12.** UNICEF	_____
4. jeep	_____	**13.** AIDS	_____
5. laser	_____	**14.** UNO	_____
6. radar	_____	**15.** TV	_____
7. MP	_____	**16.** CNN	_____
8. UNRWA	_____	**17.** UAE	_____
9. UK	_____	**18.** BBC	_____

Onomatopoeia

Another way of word formation is onomatopoeia, which results in an **onomatopoeic word**. Some call such a process **echoism**, and the resulting word is an **echoic word**, e.g., *hiss, clang (of a bell), roar*. The sounds of such words suggest their meanings. Other examples are *moan, click, murmur, whisper, quack, thunder*. Such words exist in all languages, and they are not many. In many cases, such words show some degree of similarity across different languages.

Some words show what is called **phonetic symbolism**. For example, words meaning *smoothly wet* begin in *sl-*, e.g., *slide, slush, slurp, slip, slop, slime, slick*. Another example is *fl-* (=moving light) in words like *flash, flare, flame, flicker, flimmer*. However, such symbolisms are not generally considered to be morphemes, and are sometimes called **phonesthemes**.

Exercise 5-16

Which of these words are echoic words (EW), and which ones are not echoic (NE)?

1. clink (of glasses) _____
2. sink _____
3. buzz _____
4. cuckoo _____
5. meow _____
6. whiz _____
7. fin _____
8. bleed _____
9. thunder _____
10. tick _____

Invention

Another way of word formation is invention. Some call it **word coinage**, **word manufacture**, or neologism. Such words are called **neologisms** or new words. Here, a word is totally invented from scratch to give a name for a new product of industry, e.g., *Kodak, nylon*. Names for new medicines are usually made through invention and in most cases through a computer-aided process.

Reduplication

A new word here is made by doubling a morpheme. The resulting word is called a **reduplicative** or a **twin-word**. This doubling may take one of these alternatives:

1. Repetition with no change, e.g., *pooh-pooh*.
2. Repetition with a vowel change, e.g., *pingpong*.
3. Repetition with a change of the initial consonant, e.g., *hocus-pocus*.

Exercise 5-17

What type of reduplication does each word show: no change (N), vowel change (V), or consonant change (C)? Find their meanings as well.

1. goody-goody   _____   6. seesaw   _____
2. criss-cross   _____   7. wishy-washy   _____
3. walkie-talkie   _____   8. tip-top   _____
4. din-din   _____   9. quack-quack   _____
5. tick-tock   _____   10. hubble-bubble   _____

Antonomasia

The final way of word formation is antonomasia, i.e., forming words from names of persons or places, e.g., *sandwich* after a person, *jumbo* after an elephant, *waterloo* after the Battle of Waterloo, *romeo* after Romeo, *quixotic* after Don Quixot. So are *don juan, watt, fahrenheit, xerox* (=*photocopy*). For a summary of the different processes of word formation, see Figure 5-1.

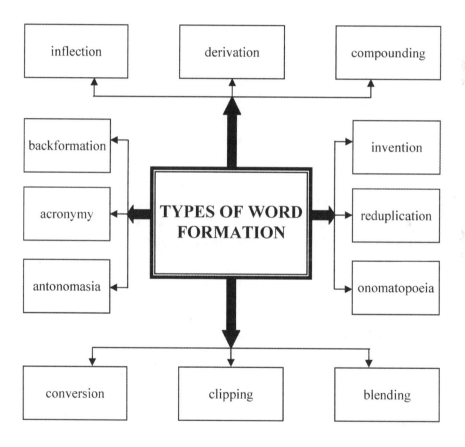

Figure 5-1: Types of Word Formation

CHAPTER 6

NOUNS

Morphology deals with two areas: word structure and word classes. Words can be classified in terms of form and function. Classification by form means that the word is classified according to its morphological structure. Such classes are called **form classes** or **morphological classes**. Classification by function is to classify the word according to its role or function inside a certain sentence. Such classes are called **functional classes** or **syntactic classes**. Some books use the term "category" instead of "class". Since this book is on morphology, we shall focus on form classes, i. e., morphological classes, and exclude functional classes, which are the main topic of syntax.

Form Classes

As for form classes, there are four **major classes**: nouns (N), adjectives (Adj), verbs (V), and adverbs (Adv). In addition, there are seven **minor classes**: prepositions (Prep), conjunctions (Con), articles (Ar), numerals (Num), pronouns (Pr), quantifiers (Q), and interjections (In). The four major classes are called **open classes**: each class includes a large number of words and allows more new words to be included. The seven minor classes are called **closed classes** because the member words are quite limited in number and the class does not allow new members.

Each form class can be identified in two ways: inflectionally or derivationally. Inflectionally, we see the inflectional suffixes that can be taken by a word, and classify it accordingly. For example, *"boy"* is a noun because it accepts the plural morpheme and the possessive morpheme, i.e., *boys, boy's*. Derivationally, we see what derivational affixes a word is taking or can take. For example, *"greatness"* is a noun because it has -*ness*.

We shall discuss these form classes in detail in this chapter and the following chapters. For an outline of form classes, see Figure 6-1.

Noun Tests

How can we decide that a certain word is a noun (N)? What distinguishes a noun from other classes? A word is a noun in these cases:

1. if it accepts the plurality morpheme, e.g., *chair(s), child(ren), datum→data,*

2. if it accepts the possessive morpheme, e.g., *man*'s, *student's,*

3. if it accepts both the plural morpheme and the possessive morpheme, e.g., *men's, teachers',*

4. if it actually ends in a noun-forming suffix, e.g., *differ<u>ence</u>, act<u>ress</u>, ideal<u>ism</u>, friend<u>ship</u>,*

5. if it can take a suffix usually added to nouns, e.g., *scholar+ship, mountain+eer, cigar+ette, lion+ess, child+ hood,*

6. or if the word belongs to a major class, but it cannot be V, Adj, or Adv. Thus, it is a N by elimination. This test is necessary for nouns that do not accept inflectional suffixes, e.g., *tennis, courage.* Such words do not accept the plural morpheme nor the possessive morpheme.

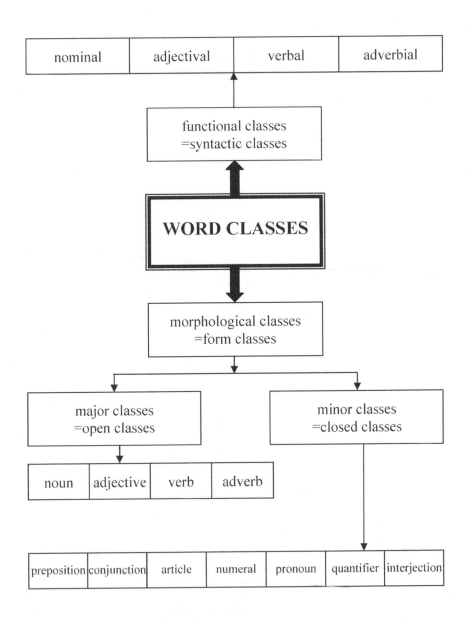

Figure 6-1: Word Classes

Exercise 6-1

Give the test number (1-6) that applies to each of these nouns, as mentioned under the subheading on "Noun Tests".

1. street   _____   **6.** curricula   _____
2. tigress   _____   **7.** John's   _____
3. boyhood   _____   **8.** payee   _____
4. girl   _____   **9.** haste   _____
5. women's   _____   **10.** farmers'   _____

Noun Forms

The noun may take one of these four forms: stem, plural, singular possessive, and plural possessive, e.g., *student, students, student's, students'*. Notice that the last three forms sound the same: they have the same pronunciation although each has a different spelling. We may call them **homophones**.

Most nouns have all the four forms, but not all nouns have these four. For example, *"man"* has four forms: *man, men, man's, men's*. Some nouns have five forms because each of them has two plurals, e.g., *brothers* and *brethren*, *fish* and *fishes*. Some nouns do not have a singular form, e.g., *clothes* and *trousers*, which are plural forms. Some nouns do not have a plural form, e.g., *physics, politics, mathematics*. Some nouns do not have a possessive form and have the *of*-structure instead, e.g., *room*, since we cannot say **the room's ceiling*, but we can say *the ceiling of the room*.

107

Exercise 6-2

Write down the other three forms of these nouns. Notice that some of these nouns may have less than four forms.

No.	Stem	Plural	Singular Possessive	Plural Possessive
1.	driver			
2.	foot			
3.	deer			
4.	Chinese			
5.	scissors			
6.	sentence			
7.	ethics			
8.	economics			
9.	Arabic			
10.	doctor			

Plural Forms

To pluralize a singular noun, if it is pluralizable, we add the **plural morpheme** to the singular form, i. e., the stem or base. This addition may take different forms and thus be realized through a variety of **allomorphs**. We may classify plurals into **regular plurals**, e.g., *books, tables, brushes*, where *s* or *es* is added, and **irregular plurals**, e.g., *sheep, children, data*.

The noun has a number, which can be either singular or plural. The test for singularity can be either the pronoun or the verb. For the singular, the pronoun *he, she,* or *it* can be used for a reference, whereas the plural takes *they*. The **singular noun** takes *is*, in contrast with the **plural noun**, which takes *are*. This test can be called **the number test**, which can be either the *he(it)/they* contrast or the *is/are* contrast. There are other possible tests of number such as the *this/these* test, the *that/those* test, the *she/they* test, the *him/them* test, the *her/them* test, and the *it/them* test.

The plural morpheme {-S₁} may have one of these allomorphs:

1. /-s/. This is added to a singular noun whose final phoneme is voiceless but not a sibilant, e.g., *book, street, top, kick*.

2. /-z/. This is added to a singular noun whose final phoneme is voiced but not a sibilant, e.g., *room, wall, stone, cover, verb, sea*.

3. /-ɨz/. This is added to a singular noun whose final phoneme is a sibilant or hissing sound, e.g., *church, bus, judge*. Sibilants are / č, ǰ, s, z, š, ž /.

4. /-z/ or **/ɨz/** + a change in the final consonant of the stem:

- /s →z/ in one word only, e.g., *hou<u>s</u>e→hou<u>s</u>es*.
- /f→v/ in about a dozen words, e.g., *kni<u>f</u>e→kni<u>v</u>es*. Other words are *half, loaf, self, wife, thief*.
- /θ→ð/ in a few words, e.g., *path→paths, mouth→mouths*. Other words are *bath, oath*.

5. /ən/. This allomorph is added to three words with or without other changes in the stem: *ox→oxen, child → children, brother→brethren*.

Thus, the plural morpheme can be expressed this way: {Plural Morpheme} = /ɨz/ ~ /s/ ~ /z/ ∞ /ən/ ∞ /Ø/, where ~

symbolizes an allomorph **phonologically conditioned**, and ∞ symbolizes an allomorph **morphologically conditioned**.

Notice that braces { } are used to include a morpheme, and slashes / / to include allomorphs, which are expressed phonemically. In linguistic symbolization, four kinds of symbols are used with four different kinds of writing:

{	}	for morphemes
/	/	for phonemes and allomorphs
[	]	for allophones
<	>	for letters or graphemes

6. The replacive allomorph. Here, an infix is used to replace the vowel in seven nouns: *man, woman, goose, tooth, foot, louse, mouse*, resulting in *men, women, geese, teeth, feet, lice, mice*. This replacement may be expressed like this: /æ→e/ for *man/men*, /uw→iy/ for *goose/geese*, /aw→ay/ for *mouse/mice*, and so on.

7. The zero allomorph. Here a Ø allomorph is added to make the plural, especially with nouns for some animals, birds, and fishes, e.g., *deer, sheep, swine, quail, bear, salmon*. Proper nouns ending in *-ese* take a zero plural allomorph also, e.g., *Japanese, Chinese*.

8. As for **foreign nouns** borrowed into English, some of them take the English plural only, e.g., *virus+es, dilemma+s, asylum+s*. Some of them take the foreign plural only, e.g., *criterion/criteria, thesis/theses, stimulus/stimuli*. The others take both plurals, i.e., English and foreign, e.g., *index→indexes or indices*. For a summary of plural forms, see Figure 6-2.

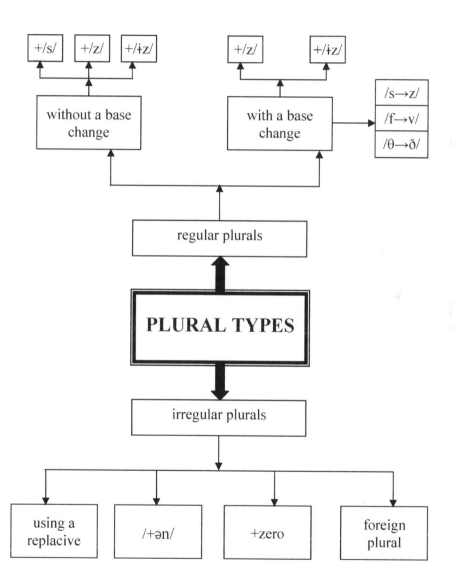

Figure 6-2: Types of Plural Forms

Exercise 6-3

Give the number of each noun: Singular (S) or plural (P), using any number test you find suitable. Some nouns can be both singular and plural (B).

1. biology   —————   6. scales   —————
2. news   —————   7. pliers   —————
3. statistic   —————   8. brethren   —————
4. ethics   —————   9. glass   —————
5. measles   —————   10. physics   —————

Exercise 6-4

Give the plural forms of these nouns, and specify the type of its plural by referring to Numbers 1-8 mentioned in the previous section.

No.	Words	Plural Form	Plural Type
1.	syllabus		
2.	basis		
3.	deer		
4.	tooth		
5.	garden		
6.	garage		
7.	tape		
8.	half		
9.	sheep		
10.	ox		

Exercise 6-5

What are the plurals of these foreign nouns as used in English? Notice that some nouns have two plurals. You may refer to the dictionary.

1. phenomenon   ————   6. formula   —————

2. stratum   ————   **7.** encyclopedia   ————
3. diagnosis   ————   **8.** museum   ————
4. erratum   ————   **9.** crisis   ————
5. memoradum   ————   **10.** datum   ————

Plural forms taking /-s, -z, -ɨz/ are **phonetically conditioned**. In other words, the quality of the final sound in the singular form determines the plural allomorph to be added, e.g., *book+/s/, dog+/z/, brush+/ɨz/*. In contrast, other varieties of plural forms are **morphologically conditioned**. In other words, there is nothing in *ox* that may lead you to predict that its plural should be *oxen*; it is an exceptional case of irregular plurality. The same is true about words like *deer, mouse,* or *foot*.

Exercise 6-6

Which of these plurals is phonetically conditioned (PC), and which is morphologically conditioned (MC)?

1. dentists   ————————   **6.** feet   ————————
2. sheep   ————————   **7.** lice   ————————
3. children   ————————   **8.** salmon   ————————
4. chiefs   ————————   **9.** circles   ————————
5. stimuli   ————————   **10.** houses   ————————

Collective Nouns

A collective noun is singular in form, but singular or plural in meaning, e.g., *class, family, team*. It refers to a group of individuals. If the speaker thinks of the group as a whole, such a noun behaves as a singular N, e.g., *The class is good*. In contrast, if he thinks of the group as separate individuals, such a N behaves as a plural N, e.g., *The class take high grades.* Other examples are *band, staff, tribe, congregation, committee, faculty.* Each of these nouns can behave as a singular N or plural N, depending on how the speaker thinks of it.

When the collective N is singular, it can be replaced by a singular pronoun (*it, its*). When it is plural, it can be replaced by a plural pronoun (*they, them, their*). Other examples of collective nouns are *public, group, government, crowd, audience.* It is obvious that a collective noun is a group of human individuals, not any group of things; it must be a group of humans.

Possessive Form

The possessive morpheme $\{-S_2\}$ added to some nouns may be realized in one of these allomorphs:

1. /-s/. This is added to a noun whose final sound is voiceless but not a sibilant, e.g., *Dick's, Robert's, the student's.*

2. /-z/. This is added to a noun whose final sound is voiced but not a sibilant, e.g., *Bob's, Edward's, the girl's, the driver's.*

3. /-ɨz/. This is added to a noun whose final sound is a sibilant, e.g., *a horse's tail, George's children.*

4. /Ø/, i.e., a zero allomorph. This is added in some expressions like *for goodness' sake, for Jesus' sake,* and is added to regular plurals as well, e.g., *the students' books.*

5. /Ø/ or /-ɨz/. Proper nouns that end in /s/ or /z/ may take either the zero allomorph or /ɨz/, e.g., *Jesus'* or *Jesus's followers, Jones'* or *Jones's dictionary.*

The possessive form is sometimes called the **genitive form**, and the possessive morpheme is sometimes called the

genitive suffix. As for spelling, it is spelled as *'s* when it is pronounced as /s, z, ɨz/ or *'* only when it is a zero allomorph, e.g., *the boy's book, the boys' books*, respectively.

Exercise 6-7

What is the possessive allomorph of each: /s, z, ɨz, or Ø/?

1. Keats's poetry	_____	6. the company's manager	_____
2. the oxen's horns	_____	7. Dick's car	_____
3. the players' luck	_____	8. the dentist's clinic	_____
4. the teachers' roles	_____	9. the village's farms	_____
5. his mother's land	_____	10. the cow's tail	_____

Meanings of the Possessive

The possessive form is used to convey several meanings or relations like these:

1. Possession, e.g., *Ali's car*

2. Description, e.g., *a summer's night*

3. Agent, e.g., *his father's approval*

4. Object, e.g., *John's punishment*

5. Origin, e.g., *Hani's letter*

6. Measure (time, value, space), e.g., *two days' holiday, a dollar's worth, two miles' distance*

Exercise 6-8

What is the meaning or relation conveyed by each of these possessive forms?

1. John's house	_____	6. a stone's throw	_____
2. Ali's question	_____	7. Dickens' novels	_____
3. the prisoner's release	_____	8. the judge's decision	_____
4. women's college	_____	9. men's coats	_____
5. ten days' absence	_____	10. Salma's bag	_____

Sometimes the possessive form may cause an ambiguity in meaning. For example, *Ali's painting* may mean possession or an agentive relation: *He is either the owner or the painter. John's examination,* another example, may mean that he is either the examiner or the examinee.

Which Nouns?

Not all nouns can take the possessive morpheme. Nouns that can take it are these:

1. Personal names, e.g., *Dick's book*

2. Personal nouns, e.g., *the boy's hat*

3. Collective nouns, e.g., *the family's future*

4. Higher animals, e.g., *the lion's share*

5. Geographical names, e.g., *London's history*

6. Institutional names, e.g., *the university's goal*

7. Measure nouns, e.g., *a week's holiday*

8. Special nouns related to human activities, e.g., *the brain's development*

Other nouns take the *of*-structure instead, e.g., *the door of the car*, not **the car's door*, or a compound form, e.g., *flower shop*.

Exercise 6-9

Justify why each possessive noun has taken the possessive morpheme, giving one of the eight types mentioned in the previous section.

1. the game's history   _____

2. Europe's future   _____

3. the nation's security   _____

4. the school's principal   _____

5. the elephant's tail   _____

6. the driver's license   _____

7. Ali's home   _____

8. an hour's break   _____

Noun-forming Suffixes

There are certain suffixes that mark nouns; we may call them **noun-markers** or noun-forming suffixes. They are added to different stems (or bases) to make nouns. Of course, we are referring here to derivational suffixes. The typical noun-forming suffixes are:

1. **-ship:** *friendship, scholarship*	N → N
2. **-ness:** *greatness, largeness*	Adj →N
3. **-age:** *coverage, postage*	V→N
4. **-ance:** *appearance, acceptance*	V→N
5. **-ion:** *dictation, composition*	V→N
6. **-ment:** *government, movement*	V→N
7. **-ist:** *dramatist, psychologist*	N→N
8. **-dom:** *kingdom, princedom*	N→N
9. **-ee:** *employee, trainee*	V→N
10. **-ence:** *dependence, difference*	V→N
11. **-eer:** *engineer, profiteer*	N→N
12. **-ess:** *actress, lioness*	N→N
13. **-ette:** *cigarette, usherette*	N→N
14. **-hood:** *childhood, boyhood*	N→N
15. **-ism:** *idealism, realism*	Adj→N
16. **-er:** *worker, farmer*	V→N
17. **-ity:** *probability, popularity*	Adj→N

There is another group of suffixes used to make the feminine form, added to the base, which is the masculine form. Such suffixes are called **femininity suffixes** or **feminizing suffixes**. These suffixes are *-e, -ess, -etta, -ina,* and *-ine*, e.g., *fiancé+e, host+ess, Henry+etta→Henrietta, George+ina→Georgina, hero+ine*. The most frequent of these suffixes is *-ess*.

In addition to these feminizing suffixes, English has about fifty words with separate feminine forms. Examples are *brother* (*sister*), *boy* (*girl*), *son* (*daughter*), *uncle* (*aunt*), *nephew* (*niece*), *monk* (*nun*), *dog* (*bitch*), *gentleman* (*lady*), *cock* (*hen*), *bachelor* (*spinster*), *man* (*woman*), *father* (*mother*), *husband* (*wife*). Some forms can be used for both masculine and feminine genders, i.e., **common gender**, e.g., *parent, friend, pupil, student, person, baby, child, teacher.*

Another group of N-forming suffixes is the suffixes of smallness or endearment, which are usually called **diminutive suffixes**. These suffixes include *-ie, -i, -y, -ette, -kin, -ikin, -ling, -et,* and *-let,* e.g., *auntie, Betty, sweetie, birdie, Johnny, dinette, lambkin, manikin, darling, duckling, circlet, booklet, starlet.*

Exercise 6-10
Give the feminine forms of these nouns.

1. prince _____	**7.** bridegroom _____
2. widower _____	**8.** landlord _____
3. tiger _____	**9.** doctor _____
4. actor _____	**10.** teacher _____
5. lad _____	**11.** trainer _____
6. lion _____	**12.** duke _____

There are, of course, other **noun-forming suffixes**, but these are the main ones. These suffixes are added to verbs, nouns, or adjectives to make nouns.

Exercise 6-11

Underline the final suffix of each word. Decide whether this suffix is a N-forming suffix (√) or not (x), and give the meaning of the suffix.

No.	Words	N-forming or not	Suffix Meaning
1.	reader		
2.	whiter		
3.	smallness		
4.	freedom		
5.	greenish		
6.	fatherhood		
7.	fatherly		
8.	different		
9.	verify		
10.	hostess		

Classification of nouns

Nouns can be either **common** or **proper**. Common nouns do not have a unique reference. They can be subdivided into **count nouns**, e.g., *chair, pen, table, room*, and **mass nouns** (or noncount nouns), e.g., *water, Arabic, oxygen, mist*.

Mass nouns include the following:
1. Whole groups, e.g., *baggage, equipment, food, fruit, furniture, jewelry, money, traffic, scenery, garbage*
2. Fluids, e.g., *water, coffee, tea*
3. Solids, e.g., *bread, iron, cotton, cheese, gold, meat*
4. Gases, e.g., *steam, oxygen, smoke, nitrogen*
5. Particles, e.g., *rice, sugar, corn, dust, flour*

6. Abstractions, e.g., *courage, justice, progress, truth, sleep*

7. Languages, e.g., *English, Arabic, French*

8. Fields of study, e.g., *biology, chemistry, economics*

9. Recreation, e.g., *chess, football, tennis*

10. General activities, e.g., *walking, studying, driving, swimming, cooking*

11. Natural phenomena, e.g., *weather, dew, fog, hail, rain, heat*

Thus, there are three sub-classes of nouns: count nouns, mass nouns, and proper nouns. Each sub-class differs from the other two in several ways (Table 6-1).

Table 6-1: Noun Sub-classes

		Plural	Numeral	many, few	much, little	Definite Article	Indefinite Article
Common	Count	+	+	+	-	+	+
	Mass	-	-	-	+	+	-
Proper		-	-	-	-	-	-

As Table 6-1 shows, count nouns can have plurals (*books*), take numerals (*two books*), take *many* and *few* (*many books*), cannot take *much* or *little* (**much books*), and can take *a* and *the*. Mass nouns (like *water*) have no plurals, take no numerals, and take neither *many* nor *a*, but they can take *much* and *the* (*much water, the water*).

In contrast, proper nouns have no plurals, and take no numerals, no *many* or *few*, no *much* or *little*, no *the*, or *a*.

Exercise 6-12

What is the subclass of each N: count N (C), mass N (M), or proper N (P)?

1. Italian _____   7. Sidney _____
2. evidence _____   8. literature _____
3. homework _____   9. grass _____
4. notebook _____   10. train _____
5. music _____   11. Makkah _____
6. walking _____   12. fire _____

Exercise 6-13

Which type of mass nouns is each of these nouns? Refer to the numbers of the eleven types in the previous section.

1. gravity _____   7. zoology _____
2. hardware _____   8. basketball _____
3. driving _____   9. milk _____
4. Spanish _____   10. smoke _____
5. beauty _____   11. wheat _____
6. silver _____   12. laughter _____

Exercise 6-14

Are these phrases right (R) or wrong (W)? Refer to Table 6-1, and know why.

1. much pens _____   6. a water _____
2. much milk _____   7. a poet _____
3. few book _____   8. few tea _____
4. the car _____   9. three fog _____
5. the London _____   10. many traffic _____

However, a mass N and a proper N can sometimes behave like a count N. Look at these pairs of examples:

1.   *He likes <u>coffee</u>. Bring two <u>coffees</u>.*
2.   *She has red <u>hair</u>. There is a <u>hair</u> here.*
3.   *<u>Shakespeare</u> was born in 1564. He is a <u>Shakespeare</u>.*

In Sentences 1-2, a mass N is used as a count N. In Sentence 3, a proper N is used as a count N.

CHAPTER 7

VERBS

In Chapter 6, we discussed the first major class of words, i.e., nouns. Here, in Chapter 7, we shall discuss another major class, i.e., verbs.

Verb Tests

How can we know that a certain word is a verb or not? Let the word undergo the verb test(s). Such tests may be derivational or inflectional.

The **derivational test** is to examine the prefix(es) or the last derivational suffix of the word. For example, *enlarge* is a verb because *en-* is a verb-forming prefix. The word *purify* is also a verb because *-ify* is a verb-forming suffix. These are examples of the derivational test of the verb.

Another supplementary or alternative way of verb testing is the **inflectional test**. Is the word taking or can it take one of the inflectional morphemes taken by the verb, i.e., the present, past, past participle, and present participle morphemes, e.g., *goes, went, gone, going*? For example, *learn*, is a verb because it can become *learns, learned, learning*. If a word passes the derivational test, the inflectional test, or both, then it belongs to the class of verbs.

Exercise 7-1
Apply the verb test, and determine whether each word is a verb (V) or not (N).

1. gather	_____	**6.** bath	_____
2. right	_____	**7.** bathe	_____
3. window	_____	**8.** teethe	_____
4. breath	_____	**9.** book	_____
5. breathe	_____	**10.** carpet	_____

Remember that many words can have a **double membership**: they can be nouns and verbs. Examples are *cord, place, ship, carpet, phrase, sentence, police, patrol, man, house, ground, land, paper*. Such words are quite abundant in English.

Verb-Forming Suffixes
English has three verb-forming suffixes: *-ify, -en,* and *-ize*. Examples are *purify, whiten, realize*. The suffix *-ify* is added to the Adj or N to make a V, e.g., *simplify, classify*. The same is true of *-en*: it is added to the Adj or N, e.g., *blacken, strengthen*. As for *-ize*, it is added to the Adj, e.g., *actualize*. In British English, both *-ise* and *-ize* are used, whereas in American English only *-ize* is used.

Verb-forming Prefixes
English has some prefixes used to make verbs from a V, N, or Adj. Here are some examples of such prefixes.

1. *un* + V → V   : *untie, undo*
2. *de* + V → V   : *defrost, degenerate*
3. *dis* + V → V   : *disconnect, disuse*
4. *mis* + V → V   : *mishear, misread*
5. *mal* + V → V   : *maltreat*

6. *out* + V → V   : *outrun, outlive*
7. *over* + V → V   : *overeat, oversleep*
8. *under* + V → V   : *undercook, underestimate*
9. *co* + V → V   : *co-operate, co-work*
10. *counter* + V → V   : *counteract, counterwork*
11. *trans* + V → V   : *transplant, transact*
12. *re* + V → V   : *re-write, re-read*
13. *be* + V → V   : *bedazzle*
    be + N → V   : *befriend*
    be + Adj → V   : *becalm*
14. *en* + Adj → V   : *enlarge, enrich*
    en + N → V   : *enslave*

Exercise 7-2

What are the verb-forming affixes in these verbs? Show their meanings.

1. undo   _____   **6.** overwork   _____
2. misinform   _____   **7.** co-manage   _____
3. outnumber   _____   **8.** entrust   _____
4. widen   _____   **9.** underachieve   _____
5. qualify   _____   **10.** disbelieve   _____

Exercise 7-3

Show the derivational rule of each verb. Example: classify = N + *ify* → V.

1. re-cycle   _____   **7.** overpay   _____
2. soften   _____   **8.** outstand   _____
3. solidify   _____   **9.** clarify   _____
4. strengthen   _____   **10.** enlist   _____
5. miscalculate   _____   **11.** ensure   _____
6. demilitarize   _____   **12.** bewitch   _____

Notice that most verb-forming prefixes do not change the class of the base. In most cases, they are added to a verb to make a verb. They only change the meaning, e.g., *understand→misunderstand*. However, some of these prefixes do change the class of the base from N or Adj into V, e.g., *befriend, becalm*.

Inflectional Suffixes

The verb may take one of these four inflectional suffixes at a time; it cannot take two of such suffixes at the same time. These suffixes are:

1.The present third-person singular suffix $\{-S_3\}$. We shall call it the **present suffix** for brevity, e.g., *goes, comes*. It is taken by the verb in the present simple tense when the subject is a third-person singular pronoun, i.e., *he, she, it*, or a singular noun. This morpheme has several allomorphs to be discussed later.

Such a morpheme is called a **portmanteau morpheme**, a term referring to a morpheme that simul-taneously represents more than one morpheme. For example, the inflectional morpheme in *goes* signals the third person, a singular subject, and the present simple tense at the same time.

2.The past suffix $\{-D_1\}$. This is added to the base to make the past from of the verb, e.g., *translated*. It has different allomorphs to be discussed later.

3.The past participle suffix $\{-D_2\}$. This is added to the base to make the past participle form, e.g., *learned, written*. It has different allomorphs as well.

4. The present participle suffix $\{-ing\}$. It is added to the base verb to make the present participle form, e.g., *going, writing, running, doing, being*. It has one allomorph, i.e., /-iŋ/. Some call it the **progressive morpheme**.

Thus, the verb has five forms: the base form, present form, past form, past participle form, and present participle form, e.g., *go, goes, went, gone, going*. The verb can take four inflectional suffixes: {-S$_3$}, {-D$_1$}, {-D$_2$}, and {-ing}.

Allomorphs of Inflectional Morphemes

Each of the verb inflectional morphemes has a variety of allomorphs. Let us discuss them one by one.

The present morpheme is symbolized as {-S$_3$} because it is similar in pronunciation and distribution to the plural morpheme {-S$_1$} and the possessive morpheme {-S$_2$}. The present morpheme has these three allomorphs:

1. /s/ if the base final sound is voiceless but not a sibilant, e.g., *meets, jumps, kicks*.

2. /z/ if the base final sound is voiced but not a sibilant, e.g., *needs, rubs, digs, boils*.

3. /ɨz/ if the base final sound is a sibilant, e.g., *washes, watches, confuses*.

The past morpheme and the past participle morpheme have these three allomorphs with regular verbs:

1. /t/ if the base final sound is voiceless but not /t/, e.g., *jumped, kicked, washed*.

2. /d/ if the base final sound is voiced but not /d/, e.g., *boiled, roamed, wandered*.

3. /ɨd/ if the base final sound is /t/ or /d/, e.g., *wanted, translated, needed, demanded*.

Of course, {-D$_1$} and {-D$_2$} have many other allomorphs with irregular verbs. Thus, {-D$_1$} can be represented this way: $\{-D_1\}$ = /t/~/d/~/ɨd/ ∞ /i→æ/ ∞ /i→ə/…etc. This formula indicates that $\{-D_1\}$ has three past allomorphs for regular verbs, all of which are phonologically conditioned, i.e., /t, d, ɨd/, e.g., *passed, learned, wanted*, respectively. It also indicates that there are other replacive allomorphs morphologically conditioned in irregular verbs, e.g., /i→æ/ as in *sing/sang*, /i→ə/ as in *sting/stung*, /ay→ow/ as in *write/wrote*, /ə→ey/ as in *become/became*, in addition to some other allomorphs used in irregular verbs.

As for $\{-D_2\}$, it has the same allomorphs as $\{-D_1\}$ with regular verbs, i.e., /t, d, ɨd/. In contrast, the $\{-D_2\}$ allomorphs with irregular verbs may generally differ from those of $\{-D_1\}$ allomorphs with some verbs, e.g., *did/done, spoke/spoken, drank/drunk, blew/blown*.

As for the progressive morpheme, i.e., the present participle morpheme $\{-ing\}$, it has one allomorph, i.e., /iŋ/, e.g., *swimming, running*.

Exercise 7-4

What is the inflectional morpheme at the end of each V: $\{-S_3\}$, $\{-D_1\}$, $\{-D_2\}$, or $\{-ing\}$? What is its allomorph?

Words	Inflectional Morpheme	Allomorph
1. maintained		
2. coming		
3. keeps		
4. uses		
5. examines		

Words	Inflectional Morpheme	Allomorph
6. placed		
7. distributed		
8. occupied		
9. sounded		
10. expecting		

Spelling of Inflectional Morphemes

The present morpheme is usually spelled as *-s* or *-es*. The *-es* spelling is found in these cases:

1. If the base final letter is *-s, -z, -ch, -sh,* or *-x,* e.g., *kiss+es, buzz+es, watch+es, brush+es, tax+es.*

2. If the base final letter is a consonant plus *-o,* e.g., *echo+es, veto+es, go+es, do+es.*

3. If the base final letter is a consonant plus *-y,* e.g., *carries, worries, cries, tries,* with *y* changed into *i.*

As for $\{-D_1\}$ and $\{-D_2\}$, the regular spelling is *-ed* or *-d.* If the base ends in a silent *-e,* we add *-d* only, e.g., *move+d, dictate+d, realize+d.* Otherwise, we add *-ed* with some changes in the base in these cases:

1. If the base ends in *-y* preceded by a consonant, *y* becomes *i,* e.g., *denied, carried, worried.*

2. If the base ends in a consonant preceded by a short vowel in a monosyllabic verb or in a final stressed syllable in a bisyllabic word, the consonant is doubled, e.g., *rub+b+ed, stop+p+ed, prefer+r+ed.*

3. If the base final letter is *-c,* it becomes *-ck,* e.g., *picnic→picnicked, traffic→trafficked.*

129

4. If the base final letter is *l* preceded by a short vowel, it is doubled, e.g., *travelled.* However, one *l* is preferred in American spelling if the second syllable is not stressed, e.g., *traveled.*

In the case of {-ing}, it is always spelled as *-ing,* with some changes in the base:

1. Doubling the final consonant as in Rule 2 of {-D$_1$} and {D$_2$}, e.g., *rubbing, swimming, admitting.*

2. Changing *c* into *ck* as in Rule 3 of {-D$_1$} and {-D$_2$}, e.g., *trafficking.*

3. Doubling the final *l* as in Rule 4 of {-D$_1$} and {-D$_2$}, e.g., *travelling* (but *traveling* in American English).

4. Dropping the final silent *e,* e.g., *move+ing→ moving.*

5. Changing the final *ie* into *y,* e.g., *die+ing→dying, lie+ing→lying.*

Exercise 7-5

Add {-S$_3$}, {-D$_1$}, and {-ing} to each following verb, observing spelling rules and exceptions. It is better to re-write the whole form.

No.	Words	{-S$_3$}	{-D$_1$}	{-ing }
1.	echo			
2.	fancy			
3.	like			
4.	rob			
5.	regret			
6.	nod			
7.	picnic			
8.	say			
9.	tie			
10.	quarrel			

Irregular Verbs

Most verbs in English are regular; we make their past form and past participle form by adding *-d* or *-ed* to the base, which makes these two forms identical, e.g., *learned, learned*. However, English has about 200 irregular verbs, whose past and past participle forms are not made by adding *-d* or *-ed*, but by infixation or vowel replacement, e.g., *speak, spoke, spoken*. Notice that most irregular verbs are monosyllabic.

Look at these examples:
1. *cut, cut, cut*
2. *begin, began, begun*
3. *find, found, found*
4. *come, came, come*

In Example (1), the base, past, and past participle have taken the same form. Other similar examples are *cost, put, set*. In Example (2), the three have taken three different forms. Other similar examples are *choose, do, go*. In Example (3), the past and the past participle are the same form, but the base is different. Other similar examples are *keep, bring, lead*. In Example (4), the base and the past participle are the same, but the past is different. More similar examples are *run, become*.

Thus, there are four patterns of irregular verbs:

1. Pattern (1) as in Example (1), tentatively symbolized as S, S, S, using S for the "*same*" and D for "*different*".
2. Pattern (2) as in Example (2), symbolized as D, D, D.
3. Pattern (3) as in Example (3), symbolized as D, S, S.
4. Pattern (4) as in example (4), symbolized as S, D, S.

Exercise 7-6

Give the past and past participle of each irregular verb, and give its pattern number.

Base	Past	Past Participle	Pattern Number
1. burst			
2. lie			
3. lead			
4. run			
5. hit			
6. wear			
7. pay			
8. swing			
9. drive			
10. shine			

Suppletion

Some irregular verbs show a phenomenon called suppletion. It is a total change of the base when an inflectional suffix is added. For example, *go* + {-D$_1$}→*went*, where there is no similarity at all between *go* and *went*. Other examples are *am, is, are, was,* and *were*, which are quite different from their base *be*. Such forms are called **suppletive forms**, and the phenomenon is called **suppletion**.

Verb Subclasses

Verbs can be classified in several ways. Most verbs are **lexical verbs**, e.g., *learn, teach, come, go*. The other subclass of verbs is **auxiliaries**, e.g., *shall, have, would*. These auxiliaries can be either modals or primaries. **Modals** are *can, could, may, might, must, shall, should, will, would,* *dare, ought to, need,* and *used to.* **Primaries** are three only: *do, have,* and *be.*

Of course, *do* includes *do, does,* and *did. Have* includes *have, has,* and *had. Be* includes *be, am, is, are, was, were, been,* and *being,* i.e., all the eight forms of the verb *be.*

Exercise 7-7

Show the subclass of each V: lexical (L), modal (M), or primary (P). Some verbs may belong to two subclasses.

1. need	_____	**6.** write	_____
2. see	_____	**7.** should	_____
3. used to	_____	**8.** could	_____
4. is	_____	**9.** do	_____
5. has	_____	**10.** may	_____

Verb Forms and Usages

As was briefly pointed out before, the verb may take five forms:

1. Base, e.g., *write*

2. Base+$\{-S_3\}$ = present simple with a third-person singular subject, e.g., *writes*

3. Base+$\{-D_1\}$ = past, e.g., *wrote*

4. Base+$\{-D_2\}$ = past participle, e.g., *written*

5. Base+$\{-ing\}$ = present participle, e.g., *writing*

The base is used in these four cases:

1. infinitive, e.g., *He can go.*

2. imperative, e.g., *Go now.*

3. present tense indicative (except with the 3rd-person singular subject), e.g., *They go to school every day.*

133

4.present tense subjunctive, e.g., *Long **live** the Mayor.*

The 3rd-person singular present is used when the verb is in the present simple, in the indicative mood, and the subject is third-person singular, e.g., *He **does** his homework regularly.*

The past form of the verb is used with the past simple tense invariably with all subjects, e.g., *He **came** yesterday.*

The past participle form is used in the passive voice, e.g., *The door was **broken**.* It is also used in the perfective aspect, e.g., *He has already **left**.* It is also used in participial structures, e.g., ***Lost** in the desert, he became almost hopeless.*

The present participle form or the progressive form is used in the progressive aspect, e.g., *He was **swimming** at that time.* It is also used in participial structures e.g., *Not **knowing** what to do, he decided to go out for a walk.*

Exercise 7-8

Which form out of these five ones is each bold-typed verb: base, third-person present, past, past participle, or present participle? What is the usage of this form?

Words	Form	Usage
1. He **arrived** last week.		
2. She can **do** it.		
3. They are **walking** now.		
4. He has **finished** his work.		
5. The job was **done**.		
6. **Knowing** the truth, he said it.		
7. It **flies** and swims.		

Words	Form	Usage
8. Sit down, please.		
9. They **feel** tired.		
10. He insists that you **be** on time.		

Aspect

Some verb forms are used to help express the aspect of the act. There are at least two aspects: the **perfective aspect** and the **progressive aspect**.

The prefective consists of two components: verb *to have* and the past participle, e.g., *have gone*. This aspect may have three varieties: the present perfective, the past perfective, and the future perfective, e.g., *has written, had written,* and *will have written*. As it is clear, each one of the three examples has verb *to have* plus the past participle.

We may add to these three perfective varieties three more. This gives us six varieties:

1. **present perfective**: *has (or have) gone*
2. **past perfective**: *had gone*
3. **future perfective**: *will have gone*
4. **present perfective progressive**: *has (or have) been going*
5. **past perfective progressive**: *had been going*
6. **future perfective progressive**: *will have been going*

The perfective aspect denotes the completion of the act before a certain point of time in the past, present, or future. Some grammarians call this aspect the **completive aspect** as well.

135

The progressive aspect denotes the continuity of the act; some grammarians call it the **continuous aspect**. This aspect must have two components: verb *to be* and the present participle. Such an aspect can be realized in six varieties, three of which are common with the perfective:

1. **prsent progressive**: *(am, is, are) writing*
2. **past progressive**: *(was, were) writing*
3. **future progressive**: *will be writing*
4. **present perfective progressive**: *has (or have) been writing*
5. **past perfective progressive**: *had been writing*
6. **future perfective progressive**: *will have been writing*

Exercise 7-9

What is the time of each V: past, present, or future? What is the aspect of each V: perfective (Per), progressive (Prog), or both (B)? What is the modal if there is any?

No.	Words	Time	Aspect	Modal
1.	will be speaking			
2.	has left			
3.	was playing			
4.	has been staying			
5.	had passed			
6.	will have finished			
7.	had been swimming			
8.	are studying			
9.	will have been reading			
10.	will be sleeping			

Voice

The past participle form is essential to make the passive voice, knowing that the V has two voices: active and passive. The **passive voice** has to have two components: verb *to be* and the past participle, e.g., *was eaten*. Notice that any form of the eight forms of the verb *be* can be used to make the passive, i.e., *be, been, being, am, is, are, was, were*. Of course, this depends on the overall structure of the verb phrase.

The verb is said to be in the **active voice** if the subject is the agent of the action, e.g., *He wrote this story*. If the subject is the recipient of the action, the verb is in the passive voice, e.g., *This story was written by him.*

Verb Phrase

The verb phrase (VP) can maximally consist of five verbs, e.g., *will have been being eaten*; however, this form is rarely used. This maximal VP consists of these units:

1. Modal. If a modal is used, it always comes initially, i.e., at the beginning of the VP, here *will*.

2. Perfective. After the modal the perfective comes, here *have been.*

3. Progressive. After the perfective we may use the progressive, here *been being*, with its two components, i.e., verb *to be* plus the present participle.

4. Passive. After the progressive, we may use the passive, here *being eaten.*

5. Lexical verb. At the end of the VP, we use the lexical verb (LV). Thus, we may have this maximal formula of the VP:

VP = (Modal) + (Perfective) + (Progressive) + (Passive) + LV

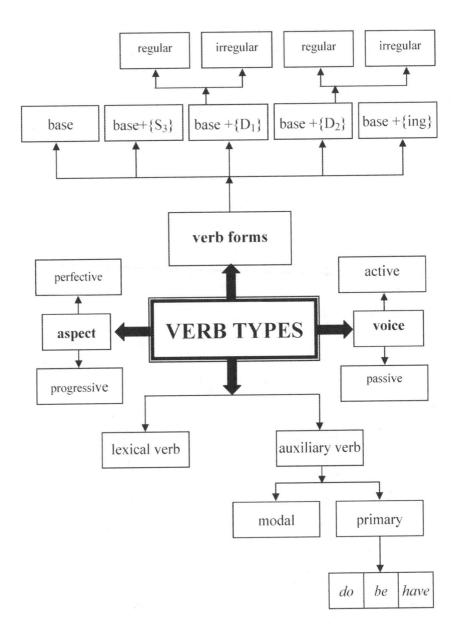

Figure 7-1: Verb Types

Notice the brackets in the formula; they are used to show option. In other words, each of the components may appear in the VP or disappear, except the LV, which is obligatory in every VP. For a summary of verb types, see Figure 7-1.

Exercise 7-10

Give an example of these verb phrases.

1. Modal+LV   _____

2. Perfective + LV   _____

3. Progressive+LV   _____

4. Passive+LV   _____

5. Modal+Passive+LV   _____

6. Modal+Perfective+LV   _____

7. Modal+Progressive+LV   _____

8. Perfective+Passive+LV   _____

9. Progressive+Passive+LV   _____

10. Modal+Perfective+Passive+LV   _____

11. Modal+Progressive+Passive+LV   _____

Exercise 7-11

Which of these sequences is grammatically correct (C) and which is incorrect (I)?

1. Perfective+Modal+LV   _____

2. LV+Progressive   _____

3. Perfective+LV   _____

4. Passive+Progressive+LV   _____

5. Perfective+Passive l LV   _____

6. Progressive+Perfective+LV   _____

7. Progressive+Passive+LV   _____

8. Passive+Modal+LV   _____

CHAPTER 8

ADJECTIVES

The adjective (Adj) is one of the major classes (or categories) of words. The other major ones are nouns, verbs, and adverbs.

Adjective Test

To test a word for being an Adj or not, we may use one of these tests:

1. The inflectional test. An Adj can take *-er*, i.e., the comparative morpheme, in many cases, e.g., *colder, hotter, smaller, larger*. You may call this test the **comparative test**. The Adj, in many cases, can also take *-est*, i.e., the superlative morpheme or the superlative suffix, e.g., *coldest, hottest, smallest, largest*. It is noticeable that if an Adj accepts *-er,* it can usually accept *-est* as well. The *-est* test can be called the **superlative test**.

2. The derivational test. There are certain suffixes that mark the Adj, e.g.,*-able, -ous, -ical, -ive, -less, -like*. If a word ends in one of these suffixes, it is an Adj, e.g., *honorable, generous, historic, economical, massive, plantless,* and *warlike*. Such a test is called the derivational test because it uses derivational suffixes.

140

3. The gradability test. Adjectives that do not accept *-er* and *-est* may accept before them gradation words like *more, most, very,* and *rather*, e.g., *more attractive, most intelligent, very interesting, rather melancholy.*

Exercise 8-1

Apply one of the Adj tests to determine whether each word is an Adj (+) or not (−). Fill in the blanks with + or − .

1. worker	_____	6. idealist	_____
2. Londoner	_____	7. careless	_____
3. clearer	_____	8. acceptable	_____
4. thoughtful	_____	9. boyish	_____
5. successive	_____	10. mature	_____

Inflectional Suffixes

Some adjectives accept *-er*, the comparative inflectional suffix, and accept *-est*, the superlative inflectional suffix, e.g., *small, smaller, smallest*. Such adjectives have three forms: the positive-degree form, e.g., *small*, the comparative-degree form, e.g., *smaller*, and the superlative-degree form, e.g., *smallest*.

The question is this: Which adjectives accept the inflectional suffixes, i.e., *-er* and *-est* for comparison? They are these adjectives:

1. Nearly all monosyllabic adjectives, e.g., *bright, fine, long, tall, wide, broad*

2. Disyllabic adjectives stressed on the second syllable, e.g., *mature, polite, sincere*

3. Disyllabic adjectives ending in *-er, -le, -ow, -ly* or *-y*, e.g., *clever, simple, narrow, friendly, happy*

141

Which adjectives take *more* and *most* for comparison? These include the following:

1. Disyllabic adjectives not stressed on the second syllable, e.g., *áncient, chármful*

2. Disyllabic adjectives not ending in *-er, -le, -ow, ly,* or *-y*, e.g., *foolish, stupid, solid, honest*

3. Participial adjectives, i.e., participles used as adjectives, e.g., *learned, blessed, charming*, which are originally past participles or present participles

4. Multisyllabic adjectives, i.e., adjectives with three syllables or more, e.g., *wonderful, beautiful, deceitful, logical*

Notice that some adjectives are not comparable because they are **non-gradable**, e.g., *circular, perfect, dead, mathematical, African, geographical*. They take neither *-er* nor *more*.

Irregular Adjectives

Some adjectives do not accept *more* (and *most)*, but they are comparable in a special irregular way. They are called irregular adjectives. Examples are:

good	*better*	*best*
bad	*worse*	*worst*
much	*more*	*most*
little	*less*	*least*
late	{ *later* / *latter* }	{ *latest* / *last* }
old	{ *older* / *elder* }	{ *oldest* / *eldest* }
far	{ *farther* / *further* }	{ *farthest* / *furthest* }

fore   *former* $\left\{\begin{array}{l} \textit{foremost} \\ \textit{first} \end{array}\right\}$

Notice that some of these irregular adjectives are **suppletive forms**, showing the phenomenon of suppletion, e.g., *better, best, worse.* Such adjectives are completely different in form from their bases. For example, *better* completely differs from the base *good;* so is *worse* in relation to *bad.* Notice that some of these irregular adjectives have regular forms as well, e.g., *late, later, latest, old, older, oldest,* with a difference in meaning.

There are some comparative adjectives without positive or superlative forms; they are irregular Latin adjectives. Examples are *superior, inferior, anterior, prior, senior, junior,* and *posterior.* They take *to,* not *than,* e.g., *He is junior to her in years, but more junior than John.*

Thus, adjectives are four types concerning comparability:
   1. Adjectives that take -*er* and -*est,* e.g., *taller, tallest*
   2. Adjectives that take *more* and *most,* e.g., *more useful, most useful*
   3. Irregular adjectives, e.g., *good, better, best*
   4. Incomparable adjectives, i.e., adjectives that cannot be logically compared, e.g., *nuclear, atomic, electrical, chemical.* These take neither -*er* nor *more.*

Exercise 8-2
   What is the type of each Adj: the -*er* type, the *more* type, the irregular type (IR), or the incomparable type (IN)?
   1. dry   _____   **6.** late   _____

2. sweet　　_____　　**7.** interested　_____

3. biological　_____　　**8.** amusing　_____

4. far　　_____　　**9.** hard　_____

5. solar　　_____　　**10.** simple　_____

Exercise 8-3

Give the comparative and superlative forms of these adjectives, using -er, -est, more, most, or irregular forms, if possible.

1. little　____　____　　**6.** young　____　____

2. only　____　____　　**7.** French　____　____

3. afraid　____　____　　**8.** ill　____　____

4. main　____　____　　**9.** medical　____　____

5. harmless　____　____　　**10.** probable　____　____

Spelling Rules

When *-er* and *-est* are added to the adjective base, some spelling rules may be observed:

1. If the base ends in *-e*, we add *-r* and *-st* only, e.g., *wide+r, wide+st, large+r, large+st.*

2. If the base ends in a single consonant preceded by a short vowel, the final consonant is doubled, e.g., *big+g+er, big+g+est, sad+d+er, sad+d+est.* Notice *sweeter, fairer.*

3. If the base ends in -y preceded by a consonant, y becomes *i* and we add *er* or *est*, e.g., *dry, drier, driest.* An exception is *shyer, shyest.* Notice *grayer, grayest.*

Exercise 8-4

Add -er and -est to these adjective bases, making any necessary spelling changes.

1. brave　____　____　　**7.** light　____　____

2. healthy　____　____　　**8.** heavy　____　____

3. dusty   ———   ———   **9.** red   ———   ———
4. gentle   ———   ———   **10.** green   ———   ———
5. angry   ———   ———   **11.** glad   ———   ———
6. near   ———   ———   **12.** hot   ———   ———

Types of Adjectives

There are different types of adjectives:

1. As for degree, there are three types of adjectives: the positive-degree Adj, the comparative-degree Adj, and the superlative-degree Adj, e.g., *small, smaller, smallest.* They can be called positive, comparative, and superlative adjectives, respectively.

2. As for form, there are two types: the **regular Adj** and the **irregular Adj**. The first type consists of the base plus *-er* or *-est*, e.g., *broader, broadest.* The second type shows a change in the base and is not a regular addition of *-er* and *-est*, e.g., *worse, worst, farther, elder.*

3. As for gradation, some adjectives are gradable. They allow intensifiers before them, i.e., words like *very, rather, fairly, somehow.* They are called **gradable adjectives** or descriptive adjectives e.g., *hot, cold, far, near, tall, short, young, old.* Other adjectives are **ungradable adjectives** or **classifying adjectives**. Such adjectives do not allow *-er, more, very,* or other intensifiers, e.g., *square, circular, geographical, equatorial, polar, oceanic, atomic, continental.*

4. As for derivation, some adjectives are derived from verbs, e.g., *charming, interesting, interested, divided, broken.* They are called **deverbal adjectives** or **participial adjectives**. They do not accept *-er* or *-est*, but they may

145

accept *more* or *most*. Some other adjectives are derived from nouns, and are thus called **denominal adjectives**, e.g., *atomic, physical, botanic, geometrical, bacterial*. Such adjectives are usually ungradable and thus accept neither *-er* nor *more*.

5. As for usage in the sentence, there are adjectives that are **attributive** only, e.g., *the main reason*; we cannot say **The reason is main*. Such adjectives are also called **limiter adjectives**. Other adjectives are **predicative** only: They come in the predicate only, e.g., *The child is awake*; we cannot say **He is an awake child*. However, most adjectives are both attributive and predicative, e.g., *green*: *It is a green car, The car is green.*

6. As for meaning, adjectives may be **stative** or **dynamic**. The stative adjective does not accept the imperative *be* or *don't be*, e.g., *tall, fat, white*. In contrast, the dynamic adjective accepts the imperative *be* or *don't be*, e.g., *careful, cruel, foolish, greedy, noisy, envious, timid, careless, brave, quiet*. Notice that most adjectives are stative and a few of them are dynamic, except for unusual purposes.

7. Proper adjectives. Such adjectives are derived from proper nouns, and are thus called proper adjectives, written in capital initials, e.g., *Jordanian, Syrian, Italian, Greek, Turkish, Iranian, Chinese.*

8. Noun adjectives. Such an adjective is a noun used as a premodifier, e.g., *a glass window, an iron door, a stone wall*. This Adj does not accept *-er* or *more*, and is used attributively only. For a brief account of adjective types, see Figure 8-1.

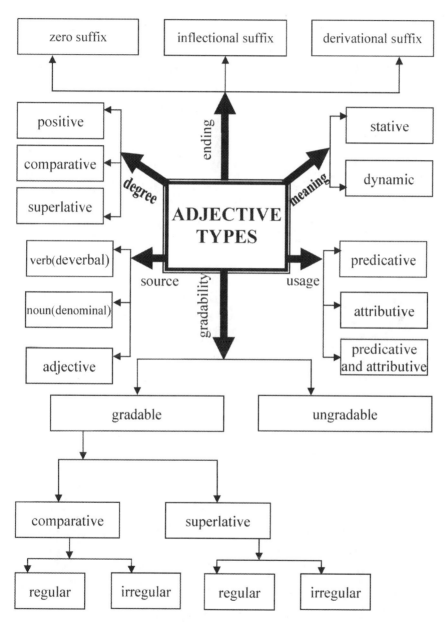

Figure 8-1: Adjective Types

Exercise 8-5

Give the type of each Adj with regard to degree: positive (P), comparative (C), or superlative (S). Determine whether it is a regular Adj (R) or an irregular Adj (IR).

1. last   _____ _____   6. highest   _____ _____
2. stronger   _____ _____   7. next   _____ _____
3. better   _____ _____   8. young   _____ _____
4. least   _____ _____   9. latter   _____ _____
5. lazy   _____ _____   10. furthest   _____ _____

Exercise 8-6

Are these adjectives gradable (G) or ungradable (UN)? Are they stative (S) or dynamic (D)?

1. generous   _____ _____   6. careless   _____ _____
2. merciful   _____ _____   7. polite   _____ _____
3. chemical   _____ _____   8. mathematical _____ _____
4. old   _____ _____   9. British   _____ _____
5. tall   _____ _____   10. courageous _____ _____

Exercise 8-7

Are these adjectives denominal (Den), deverbal (Dev), or neither (N)?

1. microbic   _____   5. triangular   _____
2. classified _____   6. circular   _____
3. spherical   _____   7. fast   _____
4. running   _____   8. gray   _____

Exercise 8-8

Are these adjectives attributive only (A), predicative only (P), or both (B)?

1. only ——————————
2. alike ——————————
3. awake ——————————
4. same ——————————
5. true ——————————

6. brave ——————————
7. former ——————————
8. ashamed ——————————
9. black ——————————
10. mere ——————————

Adjective and Prefixes

Some prefixes may be added to an adjective base to make another adjective or added to a non-adjective base to make an adjective. Such relations may be expressed by these **derivational rules**:

1. *un* + Adj → Adj : *unfair, unjust, unusual*
2. *un* + participle → Adj : *unbroken, unexpected*
3. *non* + Adj → Adj : *non-gradable, non-Islamic*
4. *in* + Adj → Adj : *incapable, invariable, invalid*
5. *dis* + Adj → Adj : *dishonest, disloyal, disgraceful*
6. *a* + Adj → Adj : *anormal, amoral*
7. *mis* + participle → Adj : *misleading, misrepresented*
8. *mal* + Adj → Adj : *malodorous, malcontent*
9. *mal* + participle → Adj : *malformed, maltreated*
10. *pseudo*+Adj→Adj : *pseudo-intellectual, pseudo-scientific, pseudo-pregnant*
11. *super*+Adj→Adj : *supernatural, superconductive, superphysical*
12. *sub* + Adj → Adj : *subnormal, subhuman, suboceanic*
13. *over*+Adj→Adj: *overconfident, overambitious, oversensitive*
14. *over*+participle→Adj : *overcrowded, overloaded, overheated*

15. *under* + participle →Adj : *underdeveloped, underplayed, undercooked*

16. *hyper* + Adj → Adj : *hypersensitive, hyperactive, hypersonic*

17. *anti* + denominal Adj → Adj: *anti-social, anti-magnetic, anti-toxic*

18. *pro* + denominal Adj →Adj: *pro-Islamic, pro-Arab, pro-German*

19. *inter*+denominal Adj→Adj: *international, intercontinental, interlinguistic*

20. *trans* + denominal Adj → Adj : *transatlantic, transnational, transpacific*

21. *pre* + Adj → Adj : *pre-marital, pre-elementary, pre-secondary, pre-natal*

22. *post* +Adj→Adj: *post-graduate, post-doctoral, postcardinal*

23. *mono* + Adj → Adj : *monolingual, monosyllabic*

24. *uni* + Adj → Adj : *unilingual, unilateral*

25. *bi* + Adj → Adj : *bilingual, bilateral*

26. *di* + Adj → Adj : *disyllabic, dipolar*

27. *tri* + Adj → Adj : *trilingual, trisyllabic*

28. *multi* + Adj → Adj: *multisyllabic, multi-racial, multinational*

29. *poly* + Adj → Adj : *polybasic, polyatomic*

Notice that the previous prefixes do not cause a change in the class of the base. They are added to adjectives to make adjectives. Even the participles mentioned in some of the previous rules are participial adjectives.

However, some prefixes are added to some bases or some adjectives to make adjectives or other classes. Here

are some of these **conversion prefixes**, i.e., prefixes that change the class of the base:
1. *be* + Adj → V : *becalm*
2. *en* + Adj → V : *enrich, enlarge*
3. *a* + V → Adj   : *awake, asleep, afloat*

All the twenty-nine rules and Rule 3 are examples of **Adj-forming prefixes** because the outputs of all these rules are adjectives.

Exercise 8-9

Write down the derivational rule of each prefixed adjective, showing the meaning of the prefix.
1. unloaded _____ un + participle → Adj _____
2. malnourished _____
3. impossible _____
4. overbusy _____
5. underprivileged _____
6. post–secondary _____
7. bimorphemic _____
8. ablaze _____
9. triangular _____
10. transoceanic _____

Adjective-forming Suffixes

There are some suffixes that mark the adjective. We can call them **Adj-forming suffixes** or **Adj markers**. Here are the typical examples of such suffixes:
1. N + *(i)an* → Adj : *Italian, African*
2. N + *ese* → Adj : *Chinese, Japanese*
3. N + *ful* → Adj   : *careful, successful*

4. N + *less* → Adj   : *stoneless, waterless*
5. N + *ly* → Adj   : *friendly, fatherly*
6. N + *like* → Adj   : *childlike, manlike*
7. N + *y* → Adj   : *windy, rainy, icy*
8. N + *ish* → Adj   : *boyish, foolish, childish*

9. N + $\begin{bmatrix} al \\ ial \\ ical \end{bmatrix}$ → Adj : *musical, editorial, historical*

10. N + *ic* → Adj : *heroic, historic, microbic*

11. N + $\begin{bmatrix} ous \\ eous \\ ious \end{bmatrix}$ → Adj : *virtuous, courteous, harmonious*

12. N + ed → Adj : *minded, hearted, carpeted*

13. Adj + ish → Adj : greenish, reddish, youngish

14. V + $\begin{bmatrix} ive \\ ative \\ itive \end{bmatrix}$ → Adj : *attractive, declarative, interrogative, sensitive*

15. V + $\begin{bmatrix} able \\ ible \end{bmatrix}$ → Adj : *readable, drinkable, comprehensible*

Exercise 8-10

Write down the derivational rule of each suffixed adjective, showing the meaning of the suffix. Example: *dependent* = V + *ent* → **Adj.**

No.	Words	Derivational Rule	Suffix Meaning
1.	Turkish		
2.	Vietnamese		
3.	flowerless		

No.	Words	Derivational Rule	Suffix Meaning
4.	drinkable		
5.	mathematical		
6.	affirmative		
7.	womanlike		
8.	wavy		

Suffixes Added to Adjectives

There are some suffixes added to adjectives to make other classes. Here is a list of some of these suffixes:

1. Adj + *ify* → V   : *simplify, clarify, purify*
2. Adj + *ize* → V   : *realize, nationalize, actualize*
3. Adj + *en* → V   : *widen, blacken, whiten*
4. Adj + *ly* → Adv : *quickly, speedily, slowly*
5. Adj + *ness* → N : *whiteness, largeness, smallness*

Exercise 8-11

Write down the derivational rule of these words, showing the meaning of the last suffix. Example: *strengthen* = N + *en* → V.

1. blackness _____ _____
2. purify _____ _____
3. carefully _____ _____
4. idealize _____ _____
5. broaden _____ _____

Compound Adjectives

If the Adj consists of one word without affixes, it is called a **simple adjective**, e.g., *hard, fast, cold*. If the Adj consists of one affixed word, it is called a **complex Adj**, e.g., *hotter, anti-magnetic*. If the Adj consists of two words, it is called a **compound Adj**. The compound adjective may take a variety of patterns:

1. Adj + N + ed : *gray-haired*
2. Adj + past participle : *low-paid*
3. Adj + N : *present-day*
4. Adv + past participle : *so-called*
5. N + present participle : *flesh-eating*
6. N + past participle : *heart-broken*
7. N + Adj : *snow-white*
8. past participle + Adv : *run-down*
9. Cardinal + N : *five-seat*

Exercise 8-12

What type is each Adj: simple (S), complex (CX), or compound (CD)?

1. new _____   5. pro-western _____
2. older _____   6. short _____
3. white-haired _____   7. shortest _____
4. short-lived _____   8. long-sighted _____

Exercise 8-13

What is the derivational pattern of each compound adjective? Choose one of the nine patterns in the previous section.

1. sky-blue _____   5. money-saving _____
2. open-minded _____   6. three-floor _____
3. well-behaved _____   7. long-live _____
4. wind-blown _____   8. raised-up _____

Adjectives as Nouns

If the Adj refers to a personal (human) quality, it may be used as a plural N if preceded by *the*, e.g., *The poor need help*. Other examples are *the rich, the young, the old, the unemployed, the deaf, the dead*. If the Adj refers to a non-personal quality, it may be used as a singular N if preceded by *the*, e.g., *The impossible has now become possible*. Other examples are *the unreal, the supernatural, the probable*. However, this rule does not apply to all adjectives. It applies only to a limited number of frequently-used adjectives.

CHAPTER 9

ADVERBS

As was mentioned before, there are four major classes of words: nouns, verbs, adjectives, and adverbs. In the previous chapters, we have presented the first three classes. In this chapter, we shall deal with the fourth class, i.e., adverbs.

Adverb-forming Suffixes

There are some suffixes that mark the adverb. They are called adverb-forming suffixes, adverb-marking suffixes, or **adverb markers**. There are five of them expressed in these derivational rules:

1. Adj + *ly* → Adv   :*slowly, carefully, gradually*
2. N + *wise* → Adv   : *studentwise, worldwise*
3. N + *ward* → Adv   : *northward, eastward*
4. N + *wards* → Adv   : *northwards, eastwards*
5. $\begin{bmatrix} N \\ Adj \end{bmatrix}$ + *like* → Adv   : *childlike, casuallike*

Notice that words like *fatherly, friendly,* and *brotherly* are adjectives, but words like *weekly, daily,* and *monthly* are both adjectives and adverbs. We have three rules here:

1. Adj + *ly* → Adv : *happily, quickly, angrily*
2. N + *ly* → Adj : *fatherly, motherly*

3. N + *ly* → Adj/Adv: *yearly, monthly*

Another point to pay attention to here is the difference between the *-ward* words and the *-wards* words, e.g., *eastward* and *eastwards*. Look at these sentences:

1. *He is going eastward (or eastwards).*
2. *He'll visit the eastward countries.*

In the adverb position, we can use either word (as in Sentence 1), but in the Adj position we cannot use except the *-ward* form (as in Sentence 2). We cannot say **the eastwards countries.*

A third important remark is about Rule 5. Words ending in *-like* can be used as adjectives and adverbs as well, e.g., *He shows a childlike behavior, He behaves childlike.*

A fourth remark is that not all adjectives can be changed to adverbs. For example, *difficult* cannot become *difficultly, but we can express the same meaning by using a phrase, e.g., *with difficulty*.

A fifth remark is that not all adverbs must end in *-ly, -ward(s), -like,* or *-wise.* Some adverbs have no suffixes at all, e.g., *fast, hard, high, late, most, right, straight, well, wide, soon.*

Exercise 9-1

Identify the adverbs in these sentences wherever they are; some sentences here do not have any adverbs.
1. He answers wisely. _____
2. He bowed low. _____

3. They went northwards.   _____

4. The upward movement was slow.   _____

5. She walks womanlike.   _____

6. He speaks very loud.   _____

7. They treated him in a friendly way.   _____

8. She worked very hard to pass the test.   _____

9. This product is used countrywise.   _____

10. He used to come early.   _____

Inflectional Suffixes

Suffixes like *-ly*, *-wise*, *-ward*, *-wards*, and *-like* are derivational suffixes. In contrast, *-er* and *-est*, which can be added to some adverbs, are inflectional suffixes, used for comparison or gradability, e.g., *hard, harder, hardest*.

These inflectional suffixes, i.e., *-er* and *-est*, are not taken by all adverbs. They are usually taken by monosyllabic adverbs, e.g., *fast, faster, fastest*. For example, **easilier* is not allowed since *easily* in not monosyllabic, whereas *earlier* is exceptionally possible. *Wrong* cannot take *-er* nor *more* because it is incomparable or ungradable.

Gradable adverbs that cannot take *-er* or *-est* may take *more* and *most*, e.g., *more easily, most easily*.

Exercise 9-2

Which of these adverbs can take *-er*, *more*, or neither?

1. near   _____   **6.** recently   _____

2. honestly   ———————   **7.** late   ———————
3. obviously   ———————   **8.** soon   ———————
4. early   ———————   **9.** right   ———————
5. loud   ———————   **10.** wrong   ———————

Spelling Rules

When we add *-er* or *-est* to the adverb base or add *-ly* to the Adj base, some spelling rules are to be observed:

1. If the base ends in *-e*, we add *-r* or *-st*, e.g., *late+r, late+st.*

2. If the base ends in *-y* preceded by a consonant and *-ly* is added, *y* is changed to *i*, e.g., *happily, merrily.*

Regular and Irregular Comparatives

Adverbs, like adjectives, have three degrees of comparison: the positive degree, the comparative degree, and the superlative degree, e.g., *fast, faster, fastest,* respectively. Adverbs of one syllable take *-er* and *-est*, and we may call them **regular adverbs**, e.g., *close, fast, hard, high, long, loud, low, slow, near, soon.* One may think that these are adjectives, not adverbs, but, in fact, they are both, e.g., *He went close* and *He is a close friend.* "Close" is an Adv in the former and an Adj in the latter.

Some adverbs show comparison inflectionally, but not in a regular way. We may call them **irregular adverbs**. Here is a list of them:

far   *farther*   *farthest*
late   *later*   *latest, last*
little   *less*   *least*

159

ill, badly	*worse*	*worst*
well	*better*	*best*
near	*nearer*	*nearest, next*

Adverbs of two syllables or more take *more* and *most*, e.g., *more directly, most directly*. Exceptions are *early, earlier, earliest* and *often, oftener*, (or *more often*), *oftenest* (or *most often*).

Notice that only gradable adverbs can be in the comparative or the superlative degrees. Adverbs like *right, wrong, perfectly*, and *circularly* cannot be but in the positive degree only.

Exercise 9-3
Give the comparative and superlative forms of these adverbs if possible.

1. humbly _____ _____
2. right _____ _____
3. close _____ _____
4. early _____ _____
5. carelessly _____ _____
6. mercifully _____ _____
7. fast _____ _____
8. far _____ _____
9. badly _____ _____
10. well _____ _____

Two-Form Adverbs
Some words have two forms of the adverb, often with different meanings. Here are some examples of such words:

    1. *He climbed <u>high</u>. I <u>highly</u> appreciate what you have done.*

    2. *He spoke <u>slow</u> (=slowly). He is a slowly dying man.*

    3. *He came <u>late</u>. He has arrived lately (=recently).*

    4. *He works <u>hard</u>. I can <u>hardly</u> (=scarcely) see him.*

    5. *He lives <u>near</u>. He has <u>nearly</u> (=almost) finished.*

Exercise 9-4

Choose the right word for each blank.

1. He answered (wrong, wrongly) _____.
2. These words are (wrong, wrongly) _____ spelled.
3. He is doing (fine, finely) _____.
4. He has (fine-, finely-) _____ cut features.
5. He stopped (short, shortly) _____.
6. He will come (short, shortly) _____.
7. He was (pretty, prettily) _____ tired.
8. She sang (pretty, prettily) _____.

Double-role Words

There are words that can be both adjectives and adverbs, depending on how they are used in the sentence:

    1. *This is a <u>high</u> building.*
    2. *The balloon went <u>high</u>.*

The word *high* is an Adj in S_1, but an Adv in S_2. Here are more examples of such words: *long, fast, right, loud, short, direct, low, late, far,* and *slow*. For a summary of adverb types, see Figure 9-1.

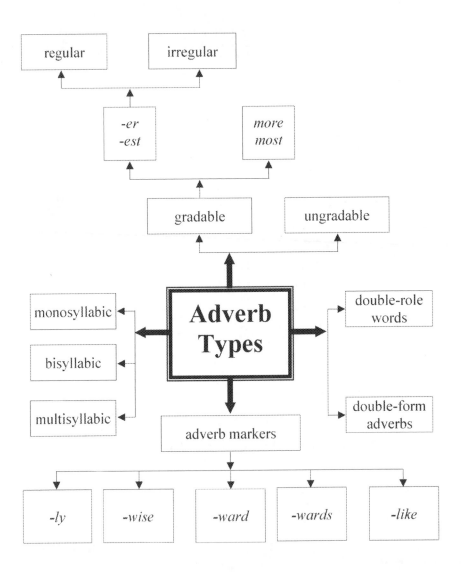

Figure 9-1: Types of Adverbs

Exercise 9-5

Use each of these words as an Adj first and then as an Adv.

1. *long* (Adj) _____
           (Adv) _____
2. *right* (Adj) _____
           (Adv) _____
3. *far* (Adj) _____
           (Adv) _____
4. *late* (Adj) _____
           (Adv) _____
5. *loud* (Adj) _____
           (Adv) _____

CHAPTER 10

MINOR CLASSES OF WORDS

Words can be classified into four **major classes**: nouns, verbs, adjectives, and adverbs, which have been discussed in detail in the last four chapters. In this chapter, we shall discuss the seven **minor classes** of words: prepositions (Prep), conjunctions (Con), articles (Ar), numerals (Num), pronouns (Pr), quantifiers (Q), and interjections (In).

There is a main difference between the four major classes of words and the seven minor classes. The major classes are **open classes**; they represent open sets of words: each class allows new words in. In contrast, the minor classes are **closed classes**: the words of each class are limited in number, and each class allows no new words in. For example, we have new nouns added to the language, but we do not have new prepositions or new conjunctions.

Prepositions
Prepositions make a closed class: no new prepositions are allowed in this class, which is limited in number.

Prepositions may consist of one word each, and such ones are called **simple prepositions**, e.g., *on, at, in, of, to, by, with, for*.

Some prepositions arc made of two or three words each and are called **compound prepositions**, e.g., *due to, in front of*. More examples of prepositions are provided in Table 10-1.

Table 10-1: Types of Prepositions

One-Word Prep	Two-Word Prep	Three-Word Prep
at	ahead of	in spite of
before	due to	with regard to
after	owing to	in front of
on	because of	in place of
of	out of	on behalf of
between	as to	in addition to
despite	as for	in case of
during	according to	by way of
from	out of	by means of
in	instead of	
until		
up		
with		
down		
like		

The most frequent prepositions are *at, by, for, from, in, of, to*, and *with*. The most frequently used Prep is *of*, then *in*, followed by *to*.

Exercise 10-1

Which of these is a simple preposition (S), compound preposition (C), or not a preposition (–)?

1. by way of	_____	**6.** round	_____
2. in light of	_____	**7.** or	_____
3. inside	_____	**8.** above	_____
4. outside	_____	**9.** under	_____
5. near	_____	**10.** nor	_____

Notice that many prepositions can be used as adverbs. Look at these sentences:

1. *He went <u>down</u> the hill. (Prep)*
2. *He went <u>down</u>. (Adv)*

Of course, the Prep needs a complement after it, called a **prepositional complement**, e.g., *He sat on <u>the chair</u>*. However, the complement may sometimes come before the Prep, e.g., <u>*What are you looking at?*</u> In some cases, the complement is optionally omitted, e.g., *This is the pen (which) you are looking for.*

Exercise 10-2

Are the bold-typed words prepositions (Prep) or adverbs (Adv)?

1. He switched **on** the radio.   _____
2. He put his hat **on**.   _____
3. He sat **on** the chair.   _____
4. She went **up** the hill.   _____
5. The smoke went **up**.   _____
6. He was reading **on**.   _____

7. They went **inside** the house.   ―――――――――――――
8. He was sitting **on** the floor.   ―――――――――――――
9. We shall meet **after**.   ―――――――――――――
10. He will come **after** seven.   ―――――――――――――

As for stress, the Prep in a sentence takes a tertiary or weak stress. In isolation, the stress of a two-syllable Prep may be on the first syllable, e.g., *únder*, or on the second syllable, e.g., *behínd*.

Exercise 10-3

Place the strong stress on the right syllable in these prepositions pronounced in isolation. Is it on the first syllable (1) or the second (2)?

1. before	――――――	**6.** below	――――――
2. about	――――――	**7.** above	――――――
3. among	――――――	**8.** against	――――――
4. after	――――――	**9.** between	――――――
5. beneath	――――――	**10.** except	――――――

Of course, prepositions have different meanings. Even a single preposition may have more than one dozen of meanings and usages. Some of them have delicate differences. Examples are:

1. *at, in: at home, in Rome.*
2. *at, on, in: at 7, on Sunday, in March.*
3. *since, for: since Friday, for three days.*
4. *beside, besides: beside me, besides this*
5. *under, below: under the table, below sea-level.*
6. *over, above: over the table, above sea-level.*
7. *in, into.*
8. *on, onto.*

Exercise 10-4

What are the differences in usage between the prepositions mentioned in the previous eight examples?

■   ■

Conjunctions

Conjunctions (Con) are a closed class of words. Concerning form, similar to prepositions, conjunctions can be **simple** if each consists of one word, e.g., *and, because, before, after, but, if, since, that, while, as, or, nor*. If the Con consists of two words or more, it is called a **compound conjunction**, e.g., *as if, as soon as, as long as, as though, so that, in case, both...and*.

Conjunctions can be **coordinators**, i.e., coordinate conjunctions, and **subordinators**, i.e., subordinate conjunctions. English has these coordinators: *and, but, or*, and *for*. Such coordinators are used to link sentences, clauses, and phrases. Other coordinators are *neither* and *nor*. In addition, there are four **correlative pairs** or correlative conjunctions: *both...and, not only...but (also), neither...nor*, and *either...or*.

As for subordinators, they are used to introduce noun clauses, e.g., *that, whether, if*, or introduce adverb clauses, e.g., *when, after, while, as, before, since, because, whereas*.

Exercise 10-5

Is each underlined word a preposition (Prep) or a conjunction (Con)?
1. He has been here <u>since</u> one.   _____

2. He couldn't come <u>since</u> he was sick.   _____

3. No one <u>but</u> him knew about it.   _____

4. He came, <u>but</u> she couldn't see him.   _____

5. She missed the bus, <u>for</u> she got up late.   _____

6. I did it only <u>for</u> you.   _____

7. He arrived <u>before</u> seven.   _____

8. She did the homework <u>before</u> she slept.   _____

9. They lined up one <u>after</u> another.   _____

10. Let me see you <u>after</u> you finish.   _____

Articles

Articles make another closed class of words. English has one **definite article**, i.e., *the*, and two **indefinite articles**, i.e., *a, an*.

If *the* is stressed, it is pronounced /ðiy/. If not stressed, it is /ðə/ before consonants, e.g., *the book*, and /ði/ before vowels, e.g., *the apple*.

As for *a* and *an*, *a* is used before consonants and *an* before vowels, e.g., *a chair, an apple*. If stressed, *a* is pronounced /ey/, e.g., á book. If unstressed, it is /ə/. If *an* is stressed, it is /æn/. If unstressed, it is /ən/.

Exercise 10-6

What kind of conjunction is each: simple (S) or compound (C), coordinator (Co) or subordinator (Sub)?

No.	Word	S or C	Co or Sub
1.	or		
2.	neither…nor		

No.	Word	S or C	Co or Sub
3.	when		
4.	as		
5.	while		
6.	nor		
7.	after		
8.	as soon as		
9.	if		
10.	but		

Numerals

Numerals make another minor class of words. They are two types: **cardinal**, e.g., *one, two, three*, and **ordinal**, e.g., *first, second, third*.

Cardinals include numbers from zero, 1, 2, 3, 4, up to infinity. **Teen numbers** (13-19) are written as one word, e.g., *thirteen, fourteen*. So are *-ty* numbers, e.g., *twenty, thirty, forty*. **Compound numbers** (21-99, except *-ty* words) are usually hyphenated, e.g., *twenty-one, twenty-two*. Numerals like *hundred, thousand*, and *million* can take *a* or *one* before them, e.g., *one (or a) hundred books*. They can also be pluralized, e.g., *many hundreds of books*, but *two hundred books*.

Ordinals are derived by adding *-th* to the cardinal, e.g., *fourth, sixth, seventh*, with changes in the base in some cases, e.g., *fifth, ninth, thirtieth*. Exceptions are *first, second, third*. They can also be written in figures like this: *1st, 2nd, 3rd, 4th, 21st, 32nd, 43rd, 55th*.

Exercise 10-7

Change these forms of cardinals from figures to letters, e.g., 30 → *thirty*.

1. 40	_____	**5.** 80	_____
2. 8	_____	**6.** 100	_____
3. 21	_____	**7.** 55	_____
4. 19	_____	**8.** 71	_____

Exercise 10-8

Change these forms of ordinals from figures to letters, e.g., 5 → *fifth*.

1. 2	_____	**6.** 46	_____
2. 51	_____	**7.** 25	_____
3. 73	_____	**8.** 1000	_____
4. 100	_____	**9.** 9	_____
5. 30	_____	**10.** 5	_____

Exercise 10-9

Put these ordinals in their correctly-spelled forms, making any necessary changes in the spelling of the base.

1. five + th =	_____	**5.** twenty + th =	_____
2. eight + th =	_____	**6.** thirty + th =	_____
3. nine + th =	_____	**7.** forty + th =	_____
4. twelve + th =	_____	**8.** seventy + th =	_____

Pronouns

Pronouns are another minor closed class, usually of one-word members. They consist of several subclasses:

1. Personal Pronouns. Personal pronouns show three **persons**: first person (*I, we*), second person (*you*), and third person (*he, she, they, it*). Personal pronouns are also marked for **case**: subjective case (*he, she, they, I*) and objective case (*him, her, them, me*). They are also marked for **number**: singular (*I, he*) and plural (*we, they*). They are marked for **gender** as well: masculine (*he*), feminine (*she*), common (*I, you, we*), and neuter (*it*).

One may notice that *you* is unmarked for gender, number, or case; it is only marked for person. *I* and *we* are unmarked for gender. The pronoun *it* is unmarked for case.

Generally speaking, a personal pronoun may be identified for person (first, second, third), for gender (masculine, feminine, neuter, common), for case (subjective, objective), and for number (singular, plural).

Exercise 10-10
Give the person, number, gender, and case of each pronoun.

No.	Word	Person	Number	Gender	Case
1.	you				
2.	him				
3.	us				
4.	they				
5.	it				
6.	she				

2. Self-pronouns. They are marked for person, number, and gender, but not for case. For example, *myself* is first person, singular, and common in gender (for masculine and feminine). Another example is *themselves*: third person, plural, and common.

Self-pronouns include *myself, yourself, himself,* and *itself* (for the singular) and *ourselves, yourselves,* and *themselves* (for the plural). They can be used emphatically and thus called **emphatic self-pronouns**, e.g., *He himself did it.* They can also be used reflexively and thus called **reflexive self-pronouns**, e.g., *He saw himself in the mirror.*

Exercise 10-11
Give the number, gender, and person of each *self-pronoun*.

No.	Word	Number	Gender	Person
1.	myself			
2.	herself			
3.	themselves			
4.	ourselves			
5.	yourselves			

3. Demonstrative pronouns. There are four of them. *This* is singular for the near. *That* is singular for the remote. *These* is plural for the near. *Those* is plural for the remote. They can stand alone or be used as part of a noun phrase, e.g., *This is incredible* or *This story is incredible.*

4. Possessive pronouns. They can be marked for person, number, and gender. For example, *his* is third person, singular, and masculine; *their* is third person, plural, and common. Possessive pronouns can be classified into two subclasses: dependent and independent. **Dependent pronouns** are *my, your, his, her, its, our, their*, e.g., *This is my book*. **Independent pronouns** are *mine, yours, his, hers, ours, theirs*, e.g., *This book is mine*.

Exercise 10-12

Show the person, number, gender, and subclass (dependent (D) or independent (I)) of each possessive pronoun.

No.	Word	Person	Number	Gender	Subclass
1.	my				
2.	his				
3.	theirs				
4.	your				
5.	her				

5. Relative pronouns. They include *who, whom, whose, which*, and *that*. They are used to introduce relative clauses, i.e., adjective clauses. Some of them are personal only (*who, whom*); some are non-personal only (*which*); some are both (*whose, that*). This personal-nonpersonal classification depends on the **antecedent** before the relative pronoun, e.g., *This is the <u>book</u> <u>which</u> I bought yesterday*.

As for dependence, all relative pronouns are used independently except *whose*, e.g., *This is the book whose cover was torn out*. As for case, *who* is subjective, *whom* objective, *which* both, *that* both, and *whose* genitive.

As for gender, all relative pronouns can be masculine, feminine, or neuter, depending on the antecedent. Their number also depends on the antecedent.

Exercise 10-13

Classify these relative pronouns for case (subjective, objective, both, genitive), number (singular, plural, both), personal / nonpersonal (or both), and dependent / independent (or both).

No.	Word	Case	Number	Personal/ Nonpersonal	Dependent/ Independent
1.	who				
2.	whom				
3.	whose				
4.	which				
5.	that				

6. Interrogative Pronouns. There are five interrogative pronouns: *who, whom, whose, what,* and *which.* They are used to introduce direct *wh*-questions and to introduce reported questions as well, e.g., *What has happened? He wants to know what has happened.*

Interrogative pronouns can refer to persons only (*who, whom, whose*) or to both persons and non-persons (*what, which*). They can also be subclassified according to their dependence. Some are used only independently (*who, whom*) and some both independently and dependently (*whose, what, which*), e.g., *Whose book is this? Whose is this book?*

7. Reciprocal pronouns. They are two: *one another* and *each other.* The subject must be plural here, e.g., *They blamed one another.*

Exercise 10-14

Classify these interrogative pronouns with regard to personal reference and dependence.

No.	Word	Personal/ Nonpersonal (P/N/Both)	Dependent/ Independent (D/I/Both)
1.	who		
2.	whom		
3.	whose		
4.	which		
5.	what		

Quantifiers

Quantifiers are a minor closed word-class. They are subclassified into three groups:

1. Group 1. This group includes the following words:

someone	*anyone*	*everyone*	*no one (none)*
somebody	*anybody*	*everybody*	*nobody*
something	*anything*	*everything*	*nothing*

This group includes three *some*-words, three *any*-words, three *every*-words, and three *no*-words. They are twelve in number. Some grammarians label them as **indefinite pronouns**. They function as heads of noun phrases, e.g., *Someone did it*.

2. Group 2. This group includes these words: *some, any, each, all, both, either, much, many (more, most), little (less, least), few (fewer, fewest), enough,* and *several*. They can function as determiners, e.g., *He needs some money*. They can also function as heads of noun phrases, e.g., *Both are coming*.

3. Group 3. This group includes *every* and *no*. They function only as determiners, e.g., *It has no effect*.

Interjections

Interjections are the last minor word-class. They are used to show emotions such as surprise, joy, pleasure, pain, or disgust. Examples are *oh, wow, ah, ugh, aha, eh,* and *damn*. For a brief account of minor word classes, see Figure 10-1.

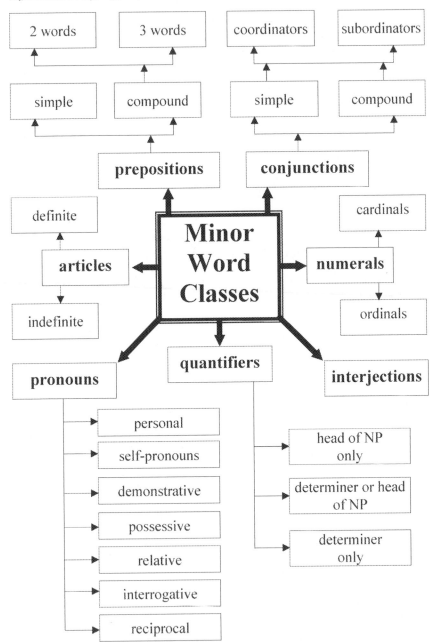

Figure 10-1: Types of Minor Word Classes

Key to Exercises

Chapter 1

Exercise 1-1:

1. re + present + ion
2. equal + ity
3. suggest + ed
4. ex + plain + ory
5. speak + er + s
6. re + search + er + s
7. con + municate + ion + s
8. con + sonant + s
9. general + ize + ion
10. develop + ment
11. Japan + ese
12. dis + cover + y

Exercise 1-2:

1. pro + cess + ed
2. con + text
3. act + ive + ate + ion
4. con + respond + s
5. in + flect + ion + al
6. de + scend + ing
7. syn + tact + ic
8. inter + pret + ion
9. pose + ion
10. un + fill + ed
11. in + form + ion
12. drama + ical + ly
13. specific + ify + s
14. accept + able + ity
15. permit + ible

Exercise 1-3:

1. /ɨz/   2. /s/   3. /z/

Exercise 1-4:

1. /ɨz/   2. /s/   3. /z/

Exercise 1-5:

1. RF	**2.** AB	**3.** AB	**4.** RB	**5.** RF
6. RB	**7.** RB	**8.** RF	**9.** AB	**10.** RF

Exercise 1-6:

1. SM	**2.** PM	**3.** SM	**4.** SM	**5.** PM
6. SM	**7.** PM	**8.** PM	**9.** PM	**10.** PM

Exercise 1-7:

1. 3M	**2.** 4M	**3.** 2M	**4.** 4M	**5.** 2M
6. 3M	**7.** 3M	**8.** 3M	**9.** 2M	**10.** 3M

Exercise 1-8:
Only roots are given here.

1. care	**2.** psyche	**3.** derive	**4.** flect	**5.** large
6. subject	**7.** denote	**8.** act	**9.** act	**10.** act

Exercise 1-9:

1. CX	**2.** S	**3.** CD	**4.** CX	**5.** CX
6. CX	**7.** CD	**8.** CD	**9.** CD	**10.** CD

Chapter 2

Exercise 2-1:

1. arch = main	**2.** be = make	**3.** bi = two
4. co = partner	**5.** de = decrease	**6.** dis = not

7. ex = previous   **8.** fore = forward   **9.** hydro = water
10. un = not

Exercise 2-2:

1. re = again   **2.** radio = ray   **3.** semi = half
4. hemi = half   **5.** sub = under   **6.** super = above
7. tele = far   **8.** trans = across   **9.** tri = three
10. ultra = above   **11.** un = not   **12.** vice = assistant
13. en = cause   **14.** en = make   **15.** in = not
16. a = on   **17.** a = in   **18.** a = not

Exercise 2-3:

1. in + Adj → Adj   **2.** in + Adj → Adj
3. mal + N → N   **4.** micro + N → N
5. milli + N → N   **6.** mis +V→V
7. multi + Adj → Adj   **8.** non + Adj → Adj
9. ploy + N → N   **10.** post + N → N

Exercise 2-4:

1. by, W   **2.** com, P   **3.** over, P   **4.** tele, P
5. in, W   **6.** in, P   **7.** self, W   **8.** under, P
9. grand, W   **10.** anti, P

Exercise 2-5:

1. not, negative prefix   **2.** against, attitude prefix
3. supporting, attitude prefix   **4.** very, degree prefix
5. not, negative prefix   **6.** wrong, pejorative prefix
7. high, degree prefix   **8.** under, locative prefix
9. not, negative prefix   **10.** wrong, pejorative prefix

Exercise 2-6:

1. half	**2.** again	**3.** not well	**4.** small	**5.** two
6. make	**7.** before	**8.** three	**9.** make	**10.** between

Exercise 2-7:

1. ing= action	**2.** ish = somewhat	**3.** ism = trend
4. ist = specialist	**5.** ish = rather	**6.** ist = player of
7. itis = infection	**8.** ize = make	**9.** less = without
10. ly = every	**11.** ly = in the manner	**12.** ment = action
13. ness = being	**14.** ous = having	**15.** ship = state of
16. ion = action	**17.** y = having	
18. wise = in the direction of		**19.** ity = being
20. ify = make		

Exercise 2-8:

1. ese	**2.** ic	**3.** ify	**4.** ish	**5.** ism	**6.** itis
7. less	**8.** ly	**9.** ist	**10.** ness	**11.** y	**12.** ion

Exercise 2-9:

1. I	**2.** D	**3.** D	**4.** I	**5.** D
6. D	**7.** D	**8.** D	**9.** D	**10.** I

Exercise 2-10:

1. N	**2.** Adj	**3.** Adj	**4.** N	**5.** N	**6.** N
7. Adj	**8.** V	**9.** N	**10.** V	**11.** N	**12.** N
13. Adv	**14.** Adj	**15.** Adv	**16.** N		

Exercise 2-11:

1. paradoxically
2. segmentalize
3. broad-minded
4. overcooked
5. implication
6. preceding
7. inferences
8. conclusion
9. exclusion
10. prefabrication
11. constraints
12. conversational
13. contextual
14. paralinguistics
15. reconstruction
16. antiglobalization
17. mispronunciation
18. miscommunication
19. non-grammaticality
20. internationalize

Exercise 2-12:

1. /aw → ay/
2. /ay → ow/
3. /ə → ey/
4. /ow → e/
5. /iy → e/
6. /uw, ow/
7. /ə → ey/
8. /i → ə/
9. /ɔw → uw/
10. /i → æ/
11. /ay → aw/
12. /ay → i/

Exercise 2-13:

1. For example, $$\left[\left[\left[\left[\text{leng}\right]+\left[\text{th}\right]\right]+\left[\text{en}\right]\right]+\left[\text{ed}\right]\right]$$

Exercise 2-14:

1. occur, occurrence, occurrent, recur, recurrent, recurrence, recurrently, etc.
   For the other words, you may refer to the dictionary.

Chapter 3

Exercise 3-1:

Follow the given example.

Exercise 3-2:

The head of the compound is the last component of each case.

Exercise 3-3:

1. 1W	2. 1W	3. 1W	4. H or 1W
5. 1W	6. H	7. 1W	8. S
9. 1W	10. 1W	11. S	12. S

Exercise 3-4:

The first units are:

1. London　　　　　**2.** police patrol　　**3.** stock market
4. electric wire　　**5.** modern language　**6.** hard cover
7. social science　　**8.** Amman

Exercise 3-5:

1. C	2. NC	3. C	4. NC	5. NC
6. C or NC, depending on meaning			7. C	8. NC
9. C	10. C	11. NC	12. NC	13. NC
14. C				

Exercise 3-6:

1. EX	2. EN	3. EX	4. EN
5. EN	6. EN	7. EX	8. EN

Exercise 3-7:

1. N	2. Adj	3. Adj	4. N	5. N
6. Adj	7. N	8. N	9. Adj	10. N

Exercise 3-8:

Examples are:
1. a quake of the earth
2. a machine used for washing
3. a writer of songs
4. an apple for cooking.

Exercise 3-9:

1. N	**2.** N	**3.** N or V	**4.** Adj	**5.** Adj
6. N	**7.** N	**8.** V	**9.** Adj	**10.** Adj

Exercise 3-10:

1. N + -ing participle	**2.** N + N
3. -ing participle + N	**4.** N + N
5. N + deverbal N	**6.** Adj + V
7. N + N	**8.** N + -ed participle
9. N + deverbal N	**10.** N + agentive N
11. N + N	**12.** N + Adj

Chapter 4

Exercise 4-1:

1. S_1	**2.** S_3	**3.** D_1 or D_2	**4.** D_1 or D_2	**5.** S_2
6. +ɨŋ	**7.** ər	**8.** əst	**9.** D_1 or D_2	**10.** +ɨŋ

Exercise 4-2:

1. D	**2.** I	**3.** N	**4.** N	**5.** I	**6.** I
7. N	**8.** N	**9.** I	**10.** I	**11.** I	**12.** I

Exercise 4-3:

1. /z/, $\{S_1\}$	**2.** /z/, $\{S_3\}$	**3.** /d/, $\{D_1\}$ or $\{D_2\}$	**4.** /ər/, {er}
5. /ɨŋ/, {ing}	**6.** /z/, $\{S_2\}$	**7.** /ɨst/, {est}	**8.** /t/, $\{D_1\}$ or $\{D_2\}$

Exercise 4-4:

1. A	**2.** C	**3.** C	**4.** R2	**5.** A
6. R_1	**7.** A	**8.** R_2	**9.** A	**10.** R_1

Exercise 4-5:

1. N	**2.** V	**3.** Adj	**4.** V	**5.** N
6. N	**7.** V	**8.** N	**9.** V	**10.** N

Exercise 4-6:

1. PP	**2.** Adj	**3.** Adj	**4.** Adj	**5.** PP
6. PP	**7.** Adj	**8.** Adj	**9.** Adj	**10.** Adj

Exercise 4-7:

1. I	**2.** I	**3.** I	**4.** R	**5.** I
6. I	**7.** I	**8.** I	**9.** I	**10.** R

Exercise 4-8:

1. -S, I, N　　**2.** -er, D, N　**3.** -ity, D, N　**4.** -er, I, Adj
5. -or, D, N　　**6.** -ess, D, N　**7.** -ous, D, Adj **8.** -ness, D, N
9. -ify, D, V　　**10.** -ing, D or I, N or V　　**11.** -ible, D, Adj
12. -ed, I, V

Chapter 5

Exercise 5-1:

1. Ø	**2.** syllabi	**3.** data	**4.** curricula
5. -s	**6.** knives	**7.** geese	**8.** -e

9. bases   **10.** criteria   **11.** theses   **12.** analyses
13. us → i   **14.** -en

Exercise 5-2:

You can refer to the dictionary to check your answers.

Exercise 5-3:

1. -er, -est   **2.** -ter, -test   **3.** better, best
4. worse, worst   **5.** y → ier, iest   **6.** -er, -est
7. -r, -st   **8.** -r, -st   **9.** –, –
10. –, –

♦ *This signal (–) here means "not possible".*

Exercise 5-4:

1. N → N   **2.** V → V   **3.** V → V
4. N → N   **5.** Adj → Adj   **6.** N → N
7. Adj → Adj   **8.** V → V   **9.** Adj → Adj
10. N → N   **11.** Adj → Adj   **12.** V → V
13. N → N   **14.** N → N   **15.** Adj → V
16. N → V

Exercise 5-5:

1. D   **2.** D   **3.** I   **4.** I   **5.** I   **6.** D
7. D   **8.** D   **9.** D   **10.** I   **11.** I   **12.** D
13. D   **14.** I

Exercise 5-6:

1. N → Adj   **2.** Adv → Adv   **3.** V → Adj
4. N → Adj   **5.** N → Adj   **6.** N → V
7. N → V   **8.** V → N   **9.** N → N
10. N → N   **11.** N → N   **12.** V → N

13. Adj → V   **14.** N → N   **15.** N → Adj
16. V → N

Exercise 5-7:

All the compounds here take this stress pattern: ´   `, i.e., a strong stress on the first component and a tertiary stress on the second component.

Exercise 5-8:

1. a. a board for writing.   b. a board that is black.
2. a. a horse for races.   b. a horse that is racing.
3. a. a room for smoking.   b. a room sending out smoke.
4. a. a teacher of French.   b. a teacher from France.
5. a. a secondary school.   b. a school high in location.

Exercise 5-9:

Different answers are possible here.

Exercise 5-10:

1. ad   **2.** math   **3.** gas   **4.** phone   **5.** lab
6. dorm   **7.** exam   **8.** mike   **9.** Fred   **10.** Al

Exercise 5-11:

1. caravan   **2.** parachute   **3.** Elizabeth
4. Antony   **5.** Joseph   **6.** Phillip
7. doctor   **8.** automobile   **9.** hamburger
10. zoological garden   **11.** facsimile   **12.** acute

Exercise 5-12:

1. escalator   **2.** transistor   **3.** smog   **4.** medicare

5. spam   **6.** motel   **7.** bit   **8.** modem
9. chunnel   **10.** brunch

Exercise 5-13:

1. resurrect   **2.** edit   **3.** wordprocess **4.** lase
5. liaise   **6.** self-destroy **7.** orate   **8.** intuit
9. hawk   **10.** televise (or televize)

Exercise 5-14:

1. -er   **2.** -r   **3.** -(e)or   **4.** -(e)ion
5. -(e)y   **6.** -ter   **7.** -gar   **8.** -or
9. -(e)or   **10.** -ance   **11.** -ion   **12.** -(e)ion

♦ *(e) here stands for "omit e".*

Exercise 5-15:

1.   oll korrect
2.   Organization of Petrol Exporting Countries
3.   white Anglo-Saxon Protestant
4.   General Purposes
5.   See the text
6.   See the text
7.   See the text
8.   United Nations Relief and Work Agency
9.   United Kingdom
10. Saudi Arabia
11. Jordanian Dinar
12. United Nations International Children's Emergency Fund
13. Acquired Immune Deficiency Syndrome
14. United Nations Organization
15. Television
16. Cable News Network
17. United Arab Emirates
18. British Broadcasting Corporation

Exercise 5-16:

1. EW	**2.** NE	**3.** EW	**4.** EW	**5.** EW
6. EW	**7.** NE	**8.** NE	**9.** EW	**10.** EW

Exercise 5-17:

1. N	**2.** V	**3.** C	**4.** N	**5.** V
6. V	**7.** V	**8.** V	**9.** N	**10.** C

Chapter 6

Exercise 6-1:

1. 1	**2.** 4	**3.** 4	**4.** 1, 2	**5.** 3
6. 1	**7.** 2	**8.** 4	**9.** 6	**10.** 3

Exercise 6-2:

1. drivers, driver's, drivers'
2. feet, —, —
3. deer, deer's, deer's
4. Chinese, —, —
5. —, —, —
6. sentences, —, —
7. —, —, —
8. —, —, —
9. —, —, —
10. doctors, doctor's, doctors'

♦ *This signal (——) here means "not possible".*

Exercise 6-3:

1. S	**2.** S	**3.** B	**4.** B	**5.** S
6. P	**7.** P	**8.** P	**9.** S	**10.** S

Exercise 6-4:

1. syllabi or syllbuses, 8   **2.** bases, 8   **3.** deer, 7   **4.** teeth, 6

5. gardens, 2   **6.** garages, 3 **7.** tapes, 1   **8.** halves, 4
9. sheep, 7   **10** oxen, 5

Exercise 6-5:

1. phenomena   **2.** strata   **3.** diagnoses   **4.** errata
5. memoranda   **6.** -e   **7.** -s   **8.** -s
9. crises   **10.** data

Exercise 6-6:

1. PC   **2.** MC   **3.** MC   **4.** PC   **5.** MC
6. MC   **7.** MC   **8.** MC   **9.** PC   **10.** PC

Exercise 6-7:

1. /ɨz/   **2.** /z/   **3.** /Ø/   **4.** /Ø/   **5.** /z/
6. /z/   **7.** /s/   **8.** /s/   **9.** /ɨz/   **10.** /z/

Exercise 6-8:

1. possession   **2.** agent   **3.** object
4. description   **5.** measure of time   **6.** measure of space
7. origin   **8.** agent   **9.** description
10. possession

Exercise 6-9:

1. 8   **2.** 5   **3.** 3   **4.** 6
5. 4   **6.** 2   **7.** 1   **8.** 7

Exercise 6-10:

1. princess   **2.** widow   **3.** tigress   **4.** actress

191

5. lass	**6.** lioness	**7.** bride	**8.** landlady
9. doctor	**10.** teacher	**11.** trainer	**12.** duchess

Exercise 6-11:

1. √, agent	**2.** ×, more	**3.** √, state	**4.** √, state
5. ×, rather	**6.** √, stage	**7.** ×, related to	**8.** ×, showing
9. ×, make	**10.** √, female		

Exercise 6-12:

1. P	**2.** M	**3.** M	**4.** C	**5.** M	**6.** M
7. P	**8.** M	**9.** M	**10.** C	**11.** P	**12.** M

Exercise 6-13:

1. 11	**2.** 1	**3.** 10	**4.** 7	**5.** 6	**6.** 3
7. 8	**8.** 9	**9.** 2	**10.** 4	**11.** 5	**12.** 6

Exercise 6-14:

1. W	**2.** R	**3.** W	**4.** R	**5.** W
6. W	**7.** R	**8.** W	**9.** W	**10.** W

Chapter 7

Exercise 7-1:

1. V	**2.** N	**3.** N	**4.** N	**5.** V
6. N	**7.** V	**8.** V	**9.** V	**10.** V

Exercise 7-2:

1. un-	**2.** mis-	**3.** out-	**4.** -en	**5.** -fy

6. over-   **7.** co-   **8.** en-   **9.** under-   **10.** dis-

Exercise 7-3:

1. re + V → V   **2.** Adj + en → V   **3.** N + ify → V
4. N + en → V   **5.** mis + V → V   **6.** de + V → V
7. over + V → V   **8.** out + V → V   **9.** Adj + ify → V
10. en + N → V   **11.** en + Adj → V   **12.** be + N → V

Exercise 7-4:

1. {-D1}, /d/   **2.** {-ing}, /ɨŋ/ **3.** {-S3}, /s/   **4.** {-S3}, /ɨz/
5. {-S3}, /z/   **6.** {-D1}, /t/ **7.** {-D1}, /ɨd/   **8.** {-D1}, /d/
9. {-D1}, /ɨd/   **10.** {-ing}, /ɨŋ/

♦ {-D1} can be {-D2} as well.

Exercise 7-5:

1. es, ed, ing   **2.** ies, ied, ing   **3.** s, d, liking
4. s, bed, bing   **5.** s, ted, ting   **6.** s, ded, ding
7. s, ked, king   **8.** s, said, ing   **9.** s, d, tying
10. s, led, ling

Exercise 7-6:

1. burst, burst, 1   **2.** lay, lain, 2   **3.** led, led, 3
4. ran, run, 4   **5.** hit, hit, 1   **6.** wore, worn, 2
7. paid, paid, 3   **8.** swung, swung, 3 **9.** drove, driven, 2
10. shone, shone, 3

Exercise 7-7:

1. L, M   **2.** L   **3.** M   **4.** L, P   **5.** L, P
6. L   **7.** M   **8.** M   **9.** L, P   **10.** M

Exercise 7-8:

1. past, indicative
2. base, infinitive
3. present, participle, progressive
4. past participle, perfective
5. past participle, passive
6. present participle, participial structure
7. present form, 3rd-person singular present
8. base, imperative
9. base, present tense
10. base, subjunctive

Exercise 7-9:

1. future, prog, will   2. present, prog, —   3. past, prog, —
4. present, B, —   5. past, per, —   6. present, per, will
7. past, B, —   8. present, prog, —   9. future, B, will
10. future, prog, will

♦ *This signal here (—) means "no modal"* .

Exercise 7-10:

Different answers may be given here.

Exercise 7-11:

1. I   2. I   3. C   4. I
5. C   6. I   7. C   8. I

Chapter 8

Exercise 8-1:

1. —   2. —   3. +   4. +   5. +

6. —   **7.** +   **8.** +   **9.** +   **10.** +

Exercise 8-2:

1. -er   **2.** -er   **3.** IN   **4.** IR   **5.** IN
6. IR, -er   **7.** more   **8.** more   **9.** -er   **10.** -er

Exercise 8-3:

1. less, least   **2.** —, —   **3.** more, most   **4.** —, —
5. more, most   **6.** -er, -est   **7.** —, —   **8.** worse, worst
9. —, —   **10.** more, most

♦ *This signal (—) means "not possible".*

Exercise 8-4:

1. r, st   **2.** y → i   **3.** y → i   **4.** r, st
5. y → i   **6.** er, est   **7.** er, est   **8.** y → i
9. dd   **10.** er, est **11.** dd   **12.** tt

Exercise 8-5:

1. S, IR   **2.** C, R   **3.** C, IR   **4.** S, IR   **5.** P, R
6. S, R   **7.** S, IR **8.** P, R   **9.** C, IR   **10.** S, IR

Exercise 8-6:

1. G, D   **2.** G, D   **3.** UN, S   **4.** G, S   **5.** G, S
6. G, D   **7.** G, D   **8.** UN, S   **9.** UN, S **10.** G, D

Exercise 8-7:

1. Den   **2.** Dev   **3.** Den   **4.** Dev
5. Den   **6.** Den   **7.** N   **8.** N

Exercise 8-8:

1. A   2. P   3. P   4. A   5. B
6. B   7. A   8. P   9. B   10. A

Exercise 8-9:

1. un + participle → Adj   2. mal + participle → Adj
3. in + Adj → Adj   4. over + Adj → Adj
5. under + participle → Adj   6. post + Adj → Adj
7. bi + Adj → Adj   8. a + V → Adj
9. tri + Adj → Adj   10. trans + Adj → Adj

Exercise 8-10:

1. N + ish → Adj   2. N + ese → Adj   3. N + less → Adj
4. V + able → Adj   5. N + ical → Adj   6. V + ative → Adj
7. N + like → Adj   8. N + y → Adj

Exercise 8-11:

1. Adj + ness → N   2. Adj + ify → V   3. Adj + ly → Adv
4. Adj + ize → V   5. Adj + en → V

Exercise 8-12:

1. S   2. CX   3. CD   4. CD
5. CX   6. S   7. CX   8. CD

Exercise 8-13:

1. 7   2. 1   3. 4   4. 6
5. 5   6. 9   7. 2   8. 8

Chapter 9

Exercise 9-1:

1. wisely   **2.** low   **3.** northwards   **4.** ——
5. womanlike   **6.** loud   **7.** ——   **8.** hard
9. countrywise   **10.** early

♦ *This signal (——) here indicates "no adverb".*

Exercise 9-2:

1. er   **2.** more   **3.** more   **4.** y → ier   **5.** er
6. more   **7.** r   **8.** er   **9.** neither   **10.** neither

Exercise 9-3:

1. more, most   **2.** ——, ——   **3.** r, st
4. y → ier, iest   **5.** more, most   **6.** more, most
7. er, est   **8.** farther, farthest   **9.** worse, worst
10. better, best

♦ *This signal (——) here indicates "not possible".*

Exercise 9-4:

1. wrongly   **2.** wrongly   **3.** fine   **4.** finely
5. short   **6.** shortly   **7.** pretty   **8.** prettily

Exercise 9-5:

Different answers here are acceptable.

Chapter 10

Exercise 10-1:

1. C   **2.** C   **3.** S   **4.** S   **5.** S

6. S   **7.** —   **8.** S   **9.** S   **10.** —

Exercise 10-2:

1. Adv   **2.** Adv   **3.** Prep   **4.** Prep   **5.** Adv
6. Adv   **7.** Prep   **8.** Prep   **9.** Adv   **10.** Prep

Exercise 10-3:

1. 2   **2.** 2   **3.** 2   **4.** 1   **5.** 2
6. 2   **7.** 2   **8.** 2   **9.** 2   **10.** 2

Exercise 10-4:

Discuss the answers with your instructor or classmates.

Exercise 10-5:

1. Prep   **2.** Con   **3.** Prep   **4.** Con   **5.** Con
6. Prep   **7.** Prep   **8.** Con   **9.** Prep   **10.** Con

Exercise 10-6:

1. S, Co   **2.** C, Co   **3.** S, Sub   **4.** S, Sub   **5.** S, Sub
6. S, Co   **7.** S, Sub   **8.** C, Sub   **9.** S, Sub   **10.** S, Co

Exercise 10-7:

1. forty   **2.** eight   **3.** twenty-one   **4.** nineteen
5. eighty   **6.** one hundred   **7.** fifty-five   **8.** seventy-one

Exercise 10-8:

1. second   **2.** fifty-first   **3.** seventy-third   **4.** hundredth

5. thirtieth	**6.** forty-sixth	**7.** twenty-fifth	**8.** thousandth
9. ninth	**10.** fifth		

Exercise 10-9:

1. fifth	**2.** eighth	**3.** ninth	**4.** twelfth
5. twentieth	**6.** thirtieth	**7.** fortieth	**8.** seventieth

Exercise 10-10:

1. second, sing & pl, common, subj & obj
2. third, singular, masculine, objective
3. first, plural, common, objective
4. third, plural, common, subjective
5. third, singular, neuter, subj & obj
6. third, singular, feminine, subjective

Exercise 10-11:

1. singular, common, first
2. singular, feminine, third
3. plural, common, third
4. plural, common, first
5. plural, common, second

Exercise 10-12:

1. first, singular, common, I
2. third, singular, masculine, D & I
3. third, plural, common, I
4. second, singular & plural, common, D
5. third, singular, feminine, D

Exercise 10-13:

1. subjective, both, personal, D   2. objective, both, personal, D

3. genitive, both, both, I   **4.** both, both, nonpersonal, D
5. both, both, both, D

Exercise 10-14:

1. P, I   **2.** P, I   **3.** P, both
4. both, both   **5.** both, both

SELECTED
BIBLIOGRAPHY

Adams, V. *An Introduction to Modern English Word-formation.* London: Longman, 1993.

Alkhuli, Muhammad Ali. *A Contrastive Transformational Grammar: Arabic and English.* The Hague: Brill, 1990.

Allen, Robert Livingston. *A Modern Grammar of Written English.* New York: Macmillan, 1995.

Anderson, J.M. *The Grammar of Case.* Cambridge: Cambridge University Press, 1991.

Aronoff, M. *Word Formation in Generative Grammar.* Cambridge, Mass: MIT Press, 1996.

Azar, B.S. *Understanding and Using English Grammar.* N.Y.: Prentice Hall, 1999.

Bach, Emmon Werner. *An Introduction to Transformational Grammars.* New York: Holt, Rinehart, and Winston, 1994.

Bauer, L. *English Word-formation.* Cambridge: Cambridge University Press, 1993.

_____. *Introducing Linguistic Morphology.* Edinbrugh: Edinbrugh Univerity Publications, 1998.

Bryant, Mar M. *A Functional English Grammar.* Boston: Heath, 1999.

Bybee, J. *Morphology: A Study of the Relation between Meaning and Form*. Amesterdam: John Benjamins, 1995.

Chomsky, N. *Reflections on Language*. New York: Pantheon, 1975.

_____. *Syntactic Structures*. The Hague: Mouton & Co., 1957.

Comrie, B. (ed.). *The World's Major Languages*. N.Y.: Oxford University Pree, 1990.

_____. *Language Universals and Linguistic Typology*. Oxford: Basil Blackwell, 1991.

Corbett, G. *Gender*. Cambridge: Cambridge University Press, 1990.

Downing, A., and P. Locke. *A University Course in English Grammar*. New York: Prentice Hall, 1992.

Dressler, W. *Morphology*. Ann Arbor: Karoma, 1995.

Elson, Benjamin, and Velma Picket. *An Introduction to Morphology and Syntax*. Santa Ana: Summer Institute of Linguistics, 1994.

Francis, Winthrop Nelson. *The Structure of American English*. New York: Ronald, 1998.

Fromkin, V., and R. Rodman. *An Introduction to Language*. N.Y.: Holt, Rinehart and Winston, 1993.

Haegeman, L. *Introduction to Government and Binding Theory*. Oxford: Blackwell, 1991.

Hammond, M. And Noonan, M. (eds). *Theoretical Morphology: Approaches in Modern Lingustics*. Orland: Academic Press, 1988.

Harris, Z. S. *Methods in Structural Linguistics*. Chicago: University of Chicago Prees; reprinted as *Structural Linguistics* (1961), 1991.

Hill, Archibald Anderson. *Introduction to Linguistic Structures: From Sound to Sentence in English.* New York: Harcourt, Brace & World, 1998.

Horrocks, G. *Generative Syntax.* London: Longman, 1987.

Joos, M. (ed). *Readings in Linguistics.* Chicago: University of Chicago Press, 1997.

Katzner, K. *The Languages of the World.* London: Routeledge & Kegan Paul, 1986.

Keyser, S.J., and P.M. Postal. *Beginning English Grammar.* N.Y.: Harper and Row, 1996.

Koutsoudas, Andreas. *Writing Transformational Grammars.* New York: Mc Graw- Hill, Inc., 1996.

Lamb, Sydney M. *Outline of Stratificational Grammar.* Washington, D.C.: Georgetown University Press, 1986.

Langacker, R.W. *Fundamentals of Linguistic Analysis.* New York: Harcourt, Brace, Jovanovich, 1992.

Long, Galph B. *The Sentence and Its Parts: A Grammar of Contemporary English.* Chicago: University of Chicago Press, 1981.

Lyons, John. *Introduction to Theoretical Linguistics.* London: Cambridge University Press, 1988.

McCawaley, J. *Grammar and Meaning.* New York : Academic Press, 1996.

Matthews, P. *Inflectional Morphology.* Cambridge: Cambridge University Press, 1992.

_____. *Morphology.* Cambridge: Cambridge University Press, 1994.

Nida, Eugene A. *Morphology: A Descriptive Analysis of Words*. 2nd ed. Ann Arbor, Mich.: University of Michigan Press, 1989.

Pence, R.W., and D. W. Emery. *A Grammar of Present-Day English*. Second Ed. New York: Macmillan, 1993.

Permutter, D. (ed). *Studies in Relational Grammar*. Chicago: University of Chicago Press, 1983.

Permutter, David M. *Deep and Surface Structure Constraints in Syntax*. New York: Holt, Rinehart, and Winston, Inc., 1991.

Postal, P. M., and P.S. Rosenbaum. *English Sentence Formation: Recent Advances in Transformational Analysis*. Mass.: Addison-Wesley, 1990.

Quirk, R., and S. Greenbaum. *A University English Grammar*. London: Longman, 1983.

Radford, A. *Transformational Grammar*. N.Y.: Cambridge Univ. Press, 1988.

Roberts, Paul. *Patterns of English*. New York: Harcourt, Brace & World, 1990.

Rogovin, Syrell. *Modern English Sentence Structure*. New York: Random House, 1984.

Sandmann, M. *Subject and Predicate*. Edinburgh: Edinburgh University Publications, 1984.

Sledd, James. *A Short Introduction to English Grammar*. Chicago: Scott and Foresman, 1999.

Spencer, A. *Morphological Theory*. London: Basil Blackwell, 1991.

Stageberg, N. C. *An Introduction to English Grammar*. New York: Holt, 1981.

Stang, Barbara M. H. *Modern English Structure*. London: Edward Arnold, 1992.

APPENDIX I
Abbreviations

Adj	adjective
Af	affix
Ar	article
Adv	adverb
CD	complementary distribution
Con	conjunction
FV	free variation
I	infix
IC	immediate constituent
In	interjection
LV	lexical verb
M	morpheme
N	noun
NP	noun phrase
Num	numeral
P	prefix
Pr	pronoun
Prep	preposition
Q	quantifier
S	suffix
V	verb
VP	verb phrase
W	word

APPENDIX III
English Phonemes

Consonants		

1. /p/ pen
2. /b/ ban
3. /t/ ten
4. /d/ down
5. /k/ kite
6. /g/ good
7. /č/ chair
8. /ǰ/ judge
9. /θ/ thin
10. /ð/ the
11. /f/ fine
12. /v/ very
13. /h/ hat
14. /s/ sign
15. /z/ zoo
16. /š/ shine
17. /ž/ treasure
18. /l/ late
19. /m/ mine
20. /n/ now
21. /ŋ/ sing
22. /w/ window
23. /r/ right
24. /y/ yet

Vowels

25. /i/ bit
26. /e/ bet
27. /æ/ hat
28. /ɨ/ wanted
29. /ə/ the
30. /a/ far
31. /u/ put
32. /ow/ boat
33. /ɔw/ bought
34. /iy/ seat
35. /ey/ same
36. /ay/ fine
37. /uw/ pool
38. /aw/ found
39. /oy/ soil

Suprasegmentals

40. / ′ / primary stress
41. / ^ / secondary stress
42. / ` / tertiary stress
43. / ˇ / weak stress
44. /+/ plus juncture
45. /→/ sustained juncture
46. /↗/ rising juncture
47. /↘/ falling juncture
48. /1/ low pitch
49. /2/ normal pitch
50. /3/ high pitch
51. /4/ extra-high pitch

Subject Index

The Author's Books

1. *A Dictionary of Islamic Terms: English-Arabic & Arabic-English*
2. *Simplified English Grammar*
3. *A Dictionary of Education: English- Arabic*
4. *A Dictionary of Theoretical Linguistics: English-Arabic*
5. *A Dictionary of Applied Linguistics: English-Arabic*
6. *Teaching English to Arab Students*
7. *A Workbook for English Teaching Practice*
8. *Programmed TEFL Methodology*
9. *The Teacher of English*
10. *Improve Your English*
11. *A Workbook for English*
12. *Advance Your English*
13. *An Introduction to Linguistics*
14. *Comparative Linguistics: English and Arabic*
15. *A Contrastive Transformational Grammar: English-Arabic*
16. *The Light of Islam*
17. *The Need for Islam*
18. *Traditions of Prophet Muhammad /B1*
19. *Traditions of Prophet Muhammad /B2*
20. *The Truth about Jesus Christ*
21. *Islam and Christianity*
22. *Questions and Answers about Islam*
23. *Learn Arabic by Yourself*
24. *The Blessing of Islam*

All the author's books may be ordered from the publisher, Dar Alfalah.

Printed in the United States
By Bookmasters